Sermons for Special Days

David G. Rogne

CSS Publishing Company
Lima, Ohio

SERMONS FOR SPECIAL DAYS

FIRST EDITION
Copyright © 2014
by CSS Publishing Co., Inc.

Published by CSS Publishing Company, Inc., Lima, Ohio 45807. All rights reserved. No part of this publication may be reproduced in any manner whatsoever without the prior permission of the publisher, except in the case of brief quotations embodied in critical articles and reviews. Inquiries should be addressed to: CSS Publishing Company, Inc., Permissions Department, 5450 N. Dixie Highway, Lima, Ohio 45807.

Some scripture quotations are from the New Revised Standard Version of the Bible. Copyright 1989 by the Division of Christian Education of the National Council of the Churches of Christ in the USA, Nashville, Thomas Nelson Publishers © 1989. Used by permission. All rights reserved.

Some scripture quotations marked are from the New English Bible. Copyright © the Delegates of the Oxford University Press and the Syndics of the Cambridge University Press, 1961, 1970. Reprinted by permission.

Library of Congress Cataloging-in-Publication Data

Rogne, David George, 1934-
  [Sermons. Selections]
  Sermons for special days / David G. Rogne. -- FIRST EDITION.
    pages cm
  ISBN 0-7880-2785-9 (alk. paper)
  1. Occasional sermons. 2. Church year sermons. I. Title.

  BV4254.2.R64 2014
  252'.97--dc23

2013050337

For more information about CSS Publishing Company resources, visit our website at www.csspub.com, email us at csr@csspub.com, or call (800) 241-4056.

e-book:
ISBN-13: 978-0-7880-2786-4
ISBN-10: 0-7880-2786-7

ISBN-13: 978-0-7880-2785-7
ISBN-10: 0-7880-2785-9

PRINTED IN USA

*This is for
Seth, Ian, Micaela,
Olivia, and Turner*

Table of Contents

New Year's Day   7
Taking Stock (Acts 24:24-27)

Mission Sunday   14
Reaching Out (Romans 10:1-15)

Heritage Sunday   20
Charles Wesley (Psalm 100)

Palm / Passion Sunday   28
Descent into Hell (1 Peter 3:18-20a; Zechariah 9:9; Luke 19:28-38)

Maundy Thursday   35
Something New (John 13:34)

Good Friday   40
It Is Finished (John 19:30)

Easter Sunday   47
Point Me Toward Tomorrow (Mark 16:1-8)

Pentecost Sunday   55
The Tower and the Flame (Genesis 11:1-9; Acts 2:1-6)

Mother's Day   62
Soul Shaping (Ephesians 6:1-4; 2 Corinthians 4:6-10)

Bible Sunday   69
Does God Have a Word for You! (2 Timothy 3:14-17)

Memorial Day   76
Heroes (Hebrews 11:1—12:2)

Music / Choir Recognition Sunday   82
Say It With Music (Ephesians 5:17-20)

Father's Day   87
Good Foundations (Ephesians 5:25—6:4)

Independence Day — 95
God's Country (1 Peter 2:9-16)

Labor Day — 101
More than Making a Living (Ecclesiates 2:18-23; John 5:17)

Stewardship Sunday — 109
Increasing the Joy (2 Corinthians 8:1-15)

World Communion Sunday — 115
Communion by the Sea (John 6:5-15, 25-35)

Reformation Day — 122
Great Scot!
John Knox (Malachi 3:1-4)

All Saints Sunday — 129
As Thousands Cheer (Hebrews 11:32—12:1)

Christ the King Sunday — 137
A Higher Loyalty (Matthew 13:31-33, 44-52)

Thanksgiving Day — 143
When the Good Times Roll (Deuteronomy 8:11-18)

Christmas Eve — 149
Are You Ready for Christmas? (Titus 2:11-15)

Christmas Day — 157
The Child with Four Names (Isaiah 9:1-7)

NEW YEAR'S DAY

Taking Stock
Acts 24:24-27

One morning when I was about six years old I was washing my face and getting ready for school, when suddenly, the water stopped running. We looked outside and saw someone from the water company turning off the water. When we complained that he ought not to be doing that, he showed us a shut-off order issued by the water company because the bill hadn't been paid. It turned out that somebody in the family was supposed to have paid the bill, but the person kept putting it off, thinking, "I'll get by there one of these days." The bill didn't get paid until late in the day, and the water didn't get turned on until the next day. From the experience, I learned the meaning of the word "procrastination."

More recently, I went to a meeting where someone gave me a paper circle with the word "tuit" printed on it. Later, the speaker described it as a round "tuit," and now that each of us had one, there was no longer a reason to put off all those things we had said we were going to do when we got "around to it." Obviously, procrastination extended beyond my family.

Once when Paul was a prisoner of the Roman government in Palestine, he was summoned before the governor, Felix, to present his case. Paul took advantage of the opportunity and commenced to preach directly to the needs of the governor. Felix became alarmed at the directness of the demands and said to Paul, "When I have a convenient season, I will call for you."

I think that remark symbolizes the tendency to procrastination with which many of us have to wrestle. It is about that tendency which I should like to speak this morning.

The first thing I would like to say is that the convenient season for many things often seems to escape us. For example, the convenient season for doing an unpleasant task may be hard to find. I read about a father who came home from work to find that his son had not finished mowing the lawn. "Tom said it was too hot to mow the lawn," the boy's mother explained. "He thinks it will be cooler when he gets back from playing tennis." Some of our justifications for not carrying out our tasks are about as sincere as that.

Sometimes the convenient season for doing something nice for someone escapes us. We have an impulse to perform a truly generous act, but this is not the appropriate moment, and soon the impulse begins to fade. One man said that whenever he had the feeling that he wanted to do some exercise he would lie down till the feeling passed. We may deal similarly with our impulses to do a good deed. The opportunity is not just right at the moment we say — we have something else to do.

Oscar Levant, after taking a good close look at himself, said in his memoirs: "Underneath this flabby exterior there is really an enormous lack of character." Perhaps that is the problem with a good many of us.

The convenient season for really living seems to elude some of us. In Meredith Wilson's *Music Man* the professor tries to get Marion the librarian to go out with him. He asks her to meet him at the footbridge across the stream running through the park. She wants to go, but she refuses. She says, "Please, some other time. Maybe tomorrow." The professor persists, yet she continues to put off their meeting. Finally, in exasperation, he says, "Pile up enough tomorrows and you'll find that you've collected nothing but a lot of empty yesterdays." Not deciding can have as much impact on our future as deciding.

The convenient season to do what we know God wants us to do never comes for some of us. E. Stanley Williamson points out that the book from which we have taken our text for today is not "The Plans and Objectives of the Apostles." The title of their story is "The Acts of the Apostles." This is so, he says, because the early followers of Jesus discovered that God's will was carried out by *doing* it, not simply *thinking* about it. When the day of judgment comes, he says we are not going to be asked what we have read, but what we have done.

Similarly, the convenient season for deciding to follow Jesus Christ never seems to come for some people. They intend to do it, but the time is never quite right. Pat Bucher spoke for a lot of people when, in a newspaper article, he said, "I'm having trouble making decisions. Last week I was at a four-way stop and spent the evening."

The governor, Felix, was having a similar problem. His name means "happy," but his life was not very happy. He is known in history for his cruelty, his tyrannical acts, his many crucifixions while he was Roman governor of Palestine. He had judged many people but Paul spoke to him of a coming judgment for *all* people and Felix began to tremble. His conscience was being touched, but Felix said, "Go away for now. When I have a convenient season I will call for you." The moment of opportunity was declined, and as far as we know, Felix never responded to the appeal he had heard.

The second thing I would like to say is that when we put off for a more convenient season something which we know we should do now, we may find that all that comes to us is the inconvenient season, when we wish desperately that we had taken care of things earlier. Failing to decide can leave us unhappy with the result.

Joseph Henry, founder of the Smithsonian Institute in Washington DC, tells a funny story on himself. When he was a boy his grandmother offered to have a pair of shoes made for him. (He lived in the era before shoe stores.) He went to a shoe cobbler, who measured his feet and he was given a choice of just two styles: square-toed or round-toed. He couldn't decide. The cobbler went ahead and started on the basic construction of the shoes and let Joseph have a couple of days to make up his mind. Joseph Henry made about half a dozen trips back to the little shoe shop over the next couple of days and still couldn't decide. On his last visit, the cobbler had a surprise for him — the shoes were finished. He handed over the finished shoes to the boy: one had a round toe; the other had a square toe. Many years later, Joseph Henry remarked, "I had to wear those monuments of indecision for a long time and they taught me, as nothing else could, the penalty one must pay for indecisiveness."

Indeed, putting off an action can lead to sorrow. There is a scene in Tolstoy's *Anna Karenina* in which Koznyshev and Varenka, two middle-aged people, are attracted to each other. Koznyshev is a scholarly fellow who is a confirmed bachelor. Varenka is a spinster who has more or less given up the possibility of marriage for herself. But she and Koznyshev have been drawn to each other and both now wonder if at long last marriage might be a possibility. One particular day the two go for a walk in the woods to hunt mushrooms. Koznyshev has already convinced himself that Varenka would be an ideal mate. He has even rehearsed his proposal and decided, on the basis of obvious signs, that Varenka would respond favorably. They walked a few steps in silence. Varenka saw that he wanted to speak; she guessed what it was about and grew faint with joy and fear. A few more minutes passed. Varenka's heart was thumping so hard that she could hear it and she felt herself turning red, then pale, then red again. To be the wife of a man like Koznyshev seemed to her the height of happiness. Besides, she was almost sure she was in love with him. And now in another moment it had to be decided. She was terrified. Terrified of what he might and what he might *not* say. Now or never was the moment when he had to make their position clear; Koznyshev, too, felt this. Everything about Varenka — her look, her blush, her lowered eyes — showed that she was in a state of painful suspense. Koznyshev saw it and was sorry for her. He quickly went over in his mind all the arguments in favor of his decision. He repeated to himself the words in which he had intended to propose to her. But instead of those words, by some sort of unaccountable idea that came into his mind, he suddenly asked: "What is the difference between a white and a birch mushroom?" Varenka's lips trembled with agitation when she replied: "There is hardly any difference in the cap. It's the stalks that are different." And the moment those words were uttered, both he and she understood that it was all over, that what should have been said would never be said, and their agitation, having reached its climax, began to subside.

Putting off our decision to know God better can also lead to the inconvenient season when we realize we have a need but we find our sensitivity to God is dulled.

Kierkegaard, the Danish philosopher, has a haunting parable concerning the wild geese that flew above his Danish countryside. One day some of the wild geese settled in a farmer's barnyard. There was much corn to be gobbled up there, so they stayed and continued to eat. They became fat and lazy. Some of their fellows flew over them and they felt the call of wild, free flight again. They extended their wings, but their heavy bodies did not rise. After a while, as they continued to live in the barnyard, it came to be that they no longer even looked up when their companions flew over. The call of the wild blue skies was no longer heard by them at all, and they were content with the mud of their existence. If we keep resisting the call, eventually we may not even hear it.

I want to say is that it is possible to avoid many of those inconvenient seasons of sorrow for what we have missed. We need to recognize our own propensity for putting things off.

The American Friends Service Committee prepared a tongue-in-cheek article advising people how to avoid making decisions based on tendencies they observed in all of us. Among the suggestions were the following:

- Profess not to have the answer; that lets you out of having any.
- Say that we must not move too rapidly; this avoids the necessity of getting started.
- Say that the problem cannot be separated from other problems. Therefore, it can't be solved until all other problems have been solved.
- Appoint a committee.
- Wait until an expert can be consulted.
- Ask what is meant by the question. By the time it is clarified, it will be time to go home.

We need to recognize that while our decisions and subsequent actions don't control everything about us, they control enough to make our choices important.

In his book *Ambition; The Secret Passion*, Joseph Epstein wrote: "We do not choose to be born. We do not choose our parents. We do not choose our historical epoch, or the country of our birth, or the immediate circumstances of our upbringing. We do not, most of us, choose to die nor do we choose the time or conditions of our death. But within all this realm of choicelessness, we do choose how we shall live: courageously or in cowardice, honorably or dishonorably, with purpose or adrift. We decide what is important and what is trivial in life. We decide that what makes us significant is either what we do or what we refuse to do. But no matter how indifferent the universe may be to our choices and decisions, these choices and decisions are ours to make. We decide. We choose. And as we decide and choose, so are our lives formed."[1]

So we need to look at our lives, decide what needs to be changed, and act on that decision. A San Francisco executive posted signs reading "Do it now!" throughout his factory, hoping to inspire his employees to action. Several weeks later, a friend asked him how his staff reacted. He shook his head in disgust: "I wish you hadn't asked. The head accountant eloped with the best secretary I ever had. Three typists asked for a raise, the factory workers voted to go on strike, and the office boy joined the Navy." Acting on our decisions may not please everybody, but *not* acting on them may keep us exactly where we've been all along.

The Bible gives us further guidance about areas of life where we need to make decisions and act on them. About work we have the words of Jesus, "I must do the works of him who sent me while it is day: the night is coming, when no one can work" (John 9:4). As we think about finding God, let us remember the words of Isaiah 55:6: "Seek the Lord while he may be found, call upon him while he is near." As we think about deciding to follow Jesus Christ, let us take to heart the words of Paul: "Behold, now is the accepted time; behold, now is the day of salvation" (2 Corinthians 6:2).

What happens when we put off making our decisions is illustrated in Sylvia Plath's novel *The Bell Jar*. Esther uses the metaphor of a fig tree to symbolize the possibilities that life holds for her. The green boughs of the tree branch out in many directions, and at the top of each branch hangs a fat purple fig. One fig represents home and children, another a career as an educator, another as a professor, and yet another as a brilliant poet. There are figs representing travel, love, adventure, and so forth. "I saw myself sitting in the crotch of this fig tree," she says, "starving to death because I couldn't make up my mind which of these figs I would choose. I wanted each and every one of them, but choosing one meant losing all the rest, and as I sat there, unable to decide, the figs began to wrinkle and go black, and, one by one, they plopped to the ground at my feet."

Today we sit at the branching point of a new year. Each of us is invited to examine our calling during the year ahead and as we look ahead, to decide what we are committed to, and what, if anything, we are going to do about it.

---

1. Joseph Epstein, *Ambition: The Secret Passion* (Chicago: Ivan R. Dee Publishing, 1989).

MISSION SUNDAY

Reaching Out
Romans 10:1-15

In his book *Unlimited Power*, Anthony Robbins tells how the accident that shut down the nuclear energy plant at Three Mile Island occurred. Many of the problems in the plant had been outlined in staff memoranda over a long period of time. As company officials later admitted, they all assumed that someone else was dealing with the matter. Instead of taking the direct steps to ask who specifically was responsible and what was being done, they assumed that someone, somewhere, was taking care of things. The result was one of the worst nuclear accidents in American history.

Getting people to accept responsibility is a key ingredient in any activity. In the passage we are looking at, the apostle Paul is looking at what he considers to be the major concern of the church — getting people saved — and through a sequence of logical steps, he tries to focus responsibility for this important work.

The first thing Paul does is to state the hoped-for end result: bringing people to salvation. I think that by that term "salvation" Paul means bringing people into a right relation with God. For Paul this is serious business because he sees people as being in jeopardy and needing help even if they don't know it. I read recently about some children who were playing in the ocean. They splashed and frolicked until all of a sudden it became clear that one of the girls was in trouble. She had drifted out beyond her depth and was fighting the waves. A lifeguard quickly spotted the danger and plunged in to help the girl, who was by now flailing, bobbing, and gasping with a wide-eyed look of panic on her face. When the guard reached her, he had to wrestle with her for a few moments, fighting his way past kicking feet and splashing arms so that he could grasp her securely and pull her safely to the shore. The girl's frantic parents rushed to embrace her and in a mixture of anxiety and relief they asked the guard, "Why did it take so long to bring her in?" The lifeguard, out of breath and panting, answered, "She was kicking so much that I couldn't get near her; we might both have been drowned. Until she stopped resisting, I had no power to help her."

What Paul sees is that each of us is flailing about trying to make some sense out of our circumstances, but often, through our own efforts, we are making our situation worse. We need to get into a right relationship with God who is waiting to help us. It calls for cooperation, not resistance.

Paul continues; to get help one must be prepared to receive it. That means recognizing that you are in trouble. A number of years ago I lived in a house which backed up against a stand of trees. The children in the neighborhood often played there, building tree houses in the tree branches. One afternoon one of the smaller boys went to play there by himself. He got up to the tree house and then decided to lower himself by tying a rope around his waist. The rope wasn't long enough to reach the ground, so he found himself dangling at the end of a rope. The more he struggled, the tighter the rope got. When he realized his predicament he began to cry for help: I heard his cry and was able to go to his aid. When things aren't going well for us — when we come to the end of our rope — we need to acknowledge our inability to set things right all by ourselves

And when we know our situation, we need to call for help. In 1942 a plane was forced down in bad weather on the Greenland icecap. Cold, snow, and the inaccessibility of the plane made the rescue of the crew unpromising. Fortunately, they had a radio in working condition, and for two days they sent out a call for help. Their signal was received, and a plane was sent to locate them, drop supplies, and begin the hunt for a way of rescue. Miraculously, after a treacherous landing on a frozen lake and twelve miles on skis, the man who finally reached them was Bernt Balchen, a noted arctic explorer, who had once saved Admiral Byrd and rescued the first German transatlantic fliers. He got them all out alive. They had to acknowledge their need, call for help, and be prepared to follow. In speaking about our human predicament, Paul, quoting an Old Testament prophet, says, "Everyone who calls on the name of the

Lord will be saved" (Romans 10:13).

However, Paul continues, if people are to be persuaded to call for help, they have to believe that help is available. People's beliefs determine their actions. I read about a woman who went to open her summer home in the mountains of Montana. Soon after she entered the house, the house caught fire. There was a public telephone nearby but she recalled that as she was driving up the mountain she had observed that the telephone line was down. So she did not call for help, and her summer home burned to the ground. She discovered later that the line had been repaired shortly after she had passed by, and she could have called for help. What we believe determines our actions.

When what we believe produces hope, we are on the way to finding our salvation. Shivering from the cold — hungry, dirty, and alone — Yuri Gevorgian slipped the noose around his neck. His dream of artistic freedom had died. He knew he couldn't survive any longer. Gevorgian had immigrated from Armenia to the United States in 1985. A successful architect, he longed to become a designer and painter. Unyielding Soviet restrictions barred him from pursuing his dreams. His best hope, he felt, was to leave the country forever. He got his wife out first. Six years after his wife moved to Southern California, Gevorgian finally got a visa. But almost as soon as he arrived at his wife's apartment, he knew the separation had been too long: His marriage had collapsed. He had to leave. Penniless and alone in a strange land, Gevorgian headed for Fresno and its large Armenian community, hoping to find help. Instead, he met with hostility from fellow countrymen who shunned him for leaving his wife. Living in doorways, he scavenged for food, trying hard to find work. His life, he thought, was ruined. In despair, he tried to hang himself. But the noose, too weak to support his body, broke and gave him back his life. Saved from death, Gevorgian was shocked into a new mission. He would make it. His journey to America couldn't be in vain. He moved to Los Angeles and found work with an architectural firm. The owner let him sleep in the office. After scraping together enough money to rent a small apartment, Gevorgian worked feverishly on a series of paintings portraying the humanity in the homeless people he had met. When a gallery owner agreed to display his work, his paintings started selling almost as quickly as they were hung. His work now fetches prices ranging from $2,500 to $200,000. "I want to keep painting and showing the beauty in people," he says. "If you have hope, you can do anything."

But to believe something, Paul points out, you have to have heard about it. If you haven't heard the offer, you don't know what is available. I attended a day-long series of lectures that were being held on the campus of the seminary I attended. I sat next to a classmate during the afternoon lecture and told him that I had missed him at the complimentary luncheon which the seminary had provided for alumni. He responded, "What luncheon?" He hadn't heard about it. Someone forgot to tell him.

People have to hear about God's love before they can accept it. Captain Edward V. Rickenbacker was America's foremost air ace in World War I. He was credited with having shot down four observation balloons and 22 enemy planes. In 1942, about a year after World War II broke out, Rickenbacker was asked by the Secretary of War, Henry Stimson, to make an inspection trip for him. On that trip over the Pacific Ocean, Eddie Rickenbacker's plane had mechanical trouble and he and the crew of seven men went down in the Pacific, 600 miles north of the Island of Samoa. For 24 days, they drifted in rubber rafts on the ocean, and the world despaired for their lives. After Captain Rickenbacker was rescued, he returned to the U.S. One day he was invited to address a large group of disabled veterans in a rehabilitation hospital. In what he said to the veterans that day, one sentence stands out above the others: "Men, if you have not had an experience of God in your life, my advice is to get busy and get yourself one. It is the one thing that will save you." This was his testimony to what had saved him, and he wanted others to hear it.

Paul points out that in his view that is the way it needs to be: If people are to hear so that they can believe, then somebody has to tell. The human instrument is important. When I was a youngster I was persuaded by my church to distribute gospel tracts — little leaflets telling people about the Christian faith. I left them on bus seats, placed them on car windshields, even attached them to helium-filled balloons. But I have come to doubt that many people come to God from something that they read. That isn't the way people are won to faith.

It is because of personal contact that most people turn to God. A pastor tells of a woman who came up to him after the service one Sunday and introduced herself as a patient who had been in a hospital room when the pastor had visited one of his members who was also in that room. "I haven't been much of a churchgoer to any great extent," she said. "I believed in God, but I was pretty vague about it all. I was to have surgery in the morning, so I was fearful, anxious, and discouraged. When I started to cry, Mary, your church member, said, 'I'm just getting ready to read my Bible and have my prayers. Maybe you would like to join me.' When we were finished she told me a little about what Jesus meant to her, and how her prayers and Bible reading and church friends gave her strength and courage. I knew then I had been missing something. I've thought about it — yes, and prayed about it, but I'm not very good at that yet. Mary invited me to church. She's waiting for me now. I want you to help me find a faith like hers." A woman's quiet testimony about what Jesus meant to her became a life-changing experience for another person and the beginning of a warm Christian friendship.

"Faith is an acoustical affair," said Martin Luther. Everyone has a message — a piece of good news to share.

Finally, Paul comes around to whose responsibility it is to get the word out. Those who have come to some understanding of God in their lives are the ones who need to tell of him. Were you afraid it was coming to that? For more than a hundred years people in the church have been singing:

I love to tell the story of unseen things above,
of Jesus and his glory, of Jesus and his love.
(Kathryn Hankey, 1868, "I Love to Tell the Story")

It's time to ask ourselves, "To whom do we love to tell it?" Moses was happily taking care of his father-in-law's sheep when he got a vision of who God was. He would have been content to keep it to himself, but God said, "Nothing doing. This has to be shared. Go down to Egypt and talk to Pharaoh." "But they won't believe me," whined Moses. "Go," said God. "But I get all tongue-tied," said Moses. "Go," said God. "Please, God, send somebody else," said Moses. "No, it's up to you," said God, "but I will be with you."

We proclaim God's love in many ways. When we demonstrate love in our actions, show concern for those who are hurting, take a stand for honesty in our relationships, offer a word of hope to the downcast, extend a hand to people in need as an expression of the love we have experienced, we are making a witness to what we believe, and every one of us has a witness to make. An elderly gentleman in the community was seen every Sunday morning walking to his church. He was completely deaf. He could not hear a word of the sermon, the music of the choir, or the hymns being sung by the congregation. One of his acquaintances wrote him a note: "Why do you spend Sundays in that church when you can't hear a word?" He replied, "I want everybody to know which side I'm on."

Each of us has our own unique message about who God is for us. If we don't share it, that one person who needs to hear it from us may never get the message. Every one of us needs to find our own way to let others know whose side we're on.

HERITAGE SUNDAY

Charles Wesley
Psalm 100

Singing of hymns will occur during the sermon.
The director should know the singing method called lining out for this sermon.

Some people have called me the sweet singer of Methodism — not because of my voice, but because God gave me the capacity to write songs. In fact, if memory serves me well, I have written some 6,000 hymns for the church. Of course, not all of them were published — only 4,430! I guess I don't know of anyone who has written more poems and hymns, though only a small number are found in any one hymnal.

Though I was inspired by God to write that many hymns, I didn't even get started in hymn writing until I was 31 years old. I had been writing poems on occasion for years, but not hymns of praise. When the Spirit got turned loose in my life, everything seemed to call forth a song.

Pardon me, here I am running on about song writing and I haven't even told you who I am. My name is Charles Wesley. My brother John and I were responsible for starting the Methodist societies. But that too gets ahead of my story. What I'd like to do right now is invite you to join your voice with mine in singing one of my hymns which has become a favorite of English-speaking Christians, "O For A Thousand Tongues To Sing."

I guess I need to go back to the beginning and tell you a little about my early years. I was born in Epworth, England, in 1707, the 18th of 19 children to be born to my parents. My mother, Susanna, was a woman of strong and forceful personality. She was intelligent, educated, energetic, pious, disciplined, and also able to fill our home with love. Please turn with me to "Love Divine, All Loves

Excelling" and join in singing the first verse so that you may begin to understand how the human love in our home prepared me to experience divine love.

My father, Samuel Wesley, was a priest in the Church of England. He was impetuous, temperamental, poetic, and humorous. I took after him; John took after my mother.

When I was about eight years old our parsonage home was destroyed by fire. John was convinced that it was arson, for there were people who were out to get my father. I mention the fire because one relic of the fire was the charred manuscript of a poem my father had written. It was set to music and has become known as "Behold The Savior Of Mankind." Listen now as it is sung. You can understand from the hymn that I came by my poetic ability naturally.

Much of my growing up took place away from home. When I was eight, I was sent to London to live with my brother, Samuel, so that I might attend school there. At thirteen I won a scholarship. At eighteen I was elected to Christ Church College, Oxford, from which my great-grandfather, my grandfather, my father, and two of my brothers had graduated. While at the University, I became more and more interested in religion. A group of us fellows gave up our earlier frivolous life and began to live by very rigid disciplines. We called ourselves "The Holy Club," but others, deriding our discipline, called us "Methodists" because we went about things methodically. When my older brother, John, returned to the University as a tutor, he gradually became the leader of our small group.

I didn't particularly want to be a clergyman, but my brother, John, who had himself become a priest, persuaded me. Neither of us was ready to pastor a church. When a friend of ours, General Oglethorpe, indicated his intention to found a colony in Georgia, in America, John and I both signed on as chaplain and missionary. Our stay in America was a very unhappy one. The settlers were generally coarse and irreligious. I am afraid that John and I had a rather severe, pietistic religion. For eighteen months I experienced privation, persecution, contempt, public disgrace, fruitless efforts, and loneliness.

I returned to England, a sick man at the age of 29. John followed a short time later. Both of us preached in the churches of some of our colleagues, but we had very little to offer, for we were ourselves seeking certainty and meaning in our faith.

Then on May 20, 1738, Pentecost, God's light somehow shone through my distress and I found the assurance of faith. Four days later, John came to my room, rejoicing, and shouting, "I believe, I believe!" for he too had found the faith. We had been trying to save our souls by rigid observances, ascetic practices, and barren legalism. Now our faith had become personal. On that very day I composed my first hymn and we sang it together. It is "Where **Shall My Wondering Soul Begin?**" God's Holy Spirit, which we proclaim in the season of Pentecost, found expression in my words. Listen as the choir sings one verse.

A year later I composed a hymn to commemorate the anniversary of our conversions; it is titled "O For A Thousand Tongues To Sing."

As I said earlier, the conversion experience unleashed the poetic muse in me to an unprecedented degree. Sometimes I would write in my study, but as I eventually traveled a great deal, many of my hymns were written on horseback. There are those who say that many of my songs have the jog-trot of a horse. Sometimes I would be deep in thought on the back of a horse and have nothing with which to write, so when I came to my destination, I would run into the house crying "pen and ink, pen and ink," and only after I had jotted down what was accumulating in my mind, would I think to greet those present.

You understand that I didn't write the music; I wrote the words. I set my words to all kinds of tunes, chanties, ballads, love songs, dance tunes, for those well-known tunes made it easy for the people to remember the words. Once I heard some sailors singing a bawdy sea chantey. I gave them some new words in praise of God, and they went away singing those. The Bible was a principal source of inspiration for me, and I guess I managed to write a hymn on practically every significant passage in the Bible. "Wrestling Jacob," or "Come O Thou Traveler Unknown," is a case in point. We will have occasion to turn to that later.

I didn't think of myself as principally a songwriter, however. Like my brother, I was a preacher. Following our conversion experiences, John and I knew we had something to share, so we became traveling evangelists, preaching in the churches when we could, and out of the church when we had to. The clergy became more and more hostile to us because our enthusiastic religion called for changed lives. Eventually, they closed their churches to us. We were determined to stay within the Church of England, and even when our converts became organized into Methodist societies for religious growth and fellowship, we were scrupulous to avoid all conflict with the schedule of the Church of England and to tell our people that they belonged within the Church of England. We saw the church as one body. Listen as one of my songs with that message, "Christ From Whom All Blessings Flow," is sung.

I traveled the length and breadth of England for eighteen years, holding meetings, preaching the gospel, and organizing societies. For ten of those years I had no home; I was constantly on the move. I traveled in rain, storms, and hurricanes. I was blown from the saddle, swamped in boats, eaten by bed bugs, squeezed in crowded accommodations. The message of God's love had been given to us. We could not let it go unproclaimed.

Not only did we have difficulty from the elements, we had great difficulty from the church. Members of the Church of England were enormously afraid that the Roman Catholic pretender to the throne was plotting to invade England and set up a Roman Catholic monarchy. Because we Methodists lived austere lives, we seemed monastic to some; because we practiced fasting, we seemed to be fanatics; because we claimed to be an order in the Church of England, people considered us to be Roman Catholic; because John governed the societies with strict authority, there were those who said he was the pope in disguise. They called him "Pope John." Because we defended Catholics when they came under attack, we were thought to be papists. Our meetings were broken up by unruly mobs throwing eggs, throwing rocks, beating drums, and making noise. Our meeting places were torn down; homes of Methodists were ransacked and burned; Methodist businesses were violently attacked, and our preachers were set upon with knives, clubs, and dogs.

All the while we were accused of trying to bring down the church. They used to say, "Charles Wesley is come to town to try, if he can, to pull the churches down." Though we considered ourselves loyal members of the Church of England, we had no protection under the law, so increasingly our Methodist preachers and preaching places had to be licensed as Dissenters, for Dissenters had protection. We published a book called *Hymns for Times of Trouble and Persecution*, to keep up the spirits of our people. One of those hymns, "Ye Servants Of God," is still preserved in some hymnals. Please turn to it with me and let us join our voices in song.

John and I found our work most readily received among the poor and needy living in the overcrowded sections of large cities. We organized societies for fellowship, classes for instruction, and preaching places where people could hear God's word proclaimed. All this was far more than two people could manage, so we made use of talented lay people who wanted the opportunity to preach. We became a highly organized, highly disciplined group of lay people in the Church of England, but the church wasn't sure it wanted us.

John and I made a good team. We had our disagreements, but we had great love and respect for each other, and we always counseled with each other so that we presented a unified front on issues. We proclaimed the same doctrines and stood together in the face of opposition. Some said that John was the head of Methodism, and that I was the heart, for John was impersonal and aloof, while I was more inclined to be warm and affectionate. In any case, we complemented each other.

Our message urged people to rejoice in God. In a moment we are going to receive the offering of the morning. We invite you to place in the offering plates your gifts for the continuing ministry of this church. As the plates are passed, let us give in the spirit of rejoicing, realizing that the Lord loves a cheerful giver. The theme of rejoicing is expressed in the hymn, "Rejoice, The Lord Is King," which the choir will sing as the offering is received.

In our Methodist societies we proclaimed salvation by faith. That means we are made right with God, not by what we do, but by what God does for us. God accepts us regardless of merit, and if we respond in repentance and faith, God comes to reside in us. Some people, including John, felt that I went too far with this thought. The idea is called mysticism: the union of the soul with God. For me the idea was very real, but John felt that it led to aberrations and individual extravagance, so he tried to edit it out of my hymns. He even denied a place in one of our hymnals to my hymn about the experience titled, "Jesus, Lover Of My Soul." Let us sing that hymn so that you may get some understanding of what I was trying to say.

Social justice was another emphasis of our message. We were ministering to the poor, so we had a great awareness of their difficulties. Where they had no medical help, we opened clinics. Where there were children without parents, we opened orphanages. Where debtors were in prison, we opened houses for the care of their families. Where there were no schools, we tried to set them up. Once we opened a school in the coal-mining area of Kingswood for the children of miners. I wrote a hymn for the service of dedication. It is titled, "Come Father, Son, And Holy Ghost." Listen as the choir sings it for us.

Another of our emphases was on free will and God's grace. We believe that God graciously invited all people to himself and that individuals were responsible for how they responded to that invitation. The Calvinists didn't see it that way. They believed that those to be saved had already been chosen by God, and that those not chosen were lost. John spoke effectively against that notion, and I wrote hymns that made our point plain. One such hymn is "Come Sinners, To The Gospel Feast." The choir director will help us to sing it by the method called "lining out."

One other point we emphasized was the possibility of perfection in this life. John felt that a relative perfection, perfection in love, was possible and felt that he had seen it in some. I felt that an absolute perfection, or holiness, was possible, but I have to confess that I never saw it. For both of us the important thing was progress — going on to perfection — to the attainment of something higher. About that possibility, I wrote the hymn, "Jesus, Thine All-Victorious Love." Let us turn to that hymn and sing it together.

Another important part of my life was the more settled role of pastor. I mentioned that I traveled for eighteen years. John continued to travel all his life. My health was not as good as his, and I longed for a more settled life. Moreover, I had married at the age of forty and needed some time with my wife and family. My wife never once complained of my being away, for she knew before we married what she was getting into. But after eight years of trying to combine marriage and travel, I felt compelled to settle down with my family.

Our work in the great metropolitan areas of London and Bristol was so large that it needed a full-time superintendent, so I took that assignment as pastor to specific congregations, while John continued to oversee the entire connection. A wealthy lady provided my wife Sally and me with a large house, and we were able to raise the three of our nine children who lived to adulthood. Our two sons, Samuel and Charles Jr. became accomplished musicians, and often gave concerts in our home, to which the nobility came.

John and I did all we could to avoid conflict with the Church of England. We avoided meeting during their hours of worship; we called our meeting places chapels, not churches; we required our people to attend the Church of England and to receive the sacraments there. But more and more our practices departed from tradition. We used extemporary prayer, we employed preaching in the fields; we administered the sacraments in places other than churches.

But the greatest bone of contention with the church was our use of lay preachers. We called a conference of Methodist preachers each year. For use on those occasions I wrote a hymn which is still sung at the opening of each Annual Conference, "And Are We Yet Alive?" Please turn to that hymn and join in singing all verses so that you may come to appreciate some of the *esprit de corps* we shared when we met. Every year the conference debated whether we should withdraw from the Church of England. Every year John and I held out. The preachers wanted ordination; they wanted to serve the sacraments. John began to vacillate. Then in 1784, without consulting with me, John ordained several people into the ministry. They were to serve in America where there would be no proper churches to provide the sacraments. As far as the Church of England was concerned, that was an act of separation. I saw it that way too and for the first time an almost irreconcilable difference occurred between John and me. John and I stayed in the Church of England, but the Methodists in America went their own way, forming a separate church. And for all practical purposes, Methodists in England gave the appearance of a separate denomination, until they too separated.

I have told you all of these things because I felt it would be well for you to become acquainted with your heritage, and because I felt that it would give you a greater appreciation for the music we share as a church. I think that each of us is involved in his or her own religious quest from birth to death, and that we benefit from the experiences of one another. In a moment we will have occasion to sing a hymn about that religious experience, "Come, O Thou Traveler Unknown," but first let us bow in prayer, as our service is brought to a close.

PALM / PASSION SUNDAY

Descent into Hell
1 Peter 3:18-20a; Zechariah 9:9; Luke 19:28-38

When Abraham Lincoln's body was brought from Washington to Illinois, it passed through Albany and, as it was carried through the street, they say a black woman stood on the curb and lifted her little son as far as she could reach above the heads of the crowd. She was heard to say to him, "Take a long look, honey, he died for you." He died for you! That is what Christians have been saying about Jesus Christ! Early Christians, believing that something important was accomplished by the passion of Christ, included in the Apostles' Creed the reminder that Jesus "suffered, was crucified, dead and buried"; and there is that intriguing footnote indicated by an asterisk in our version of the Creed: "He descended into hell." Today I would like us to think about why it was necessary for Christ to suffer.

The first aspect of his suffering that I would like us to consider is the last element in this string of references in the Apostles' Creed to the passion of Christ: "He descended into hell." It is evident that since this item is now a footnote in our version, some Christians who dealt with this creed must have had trouble with these words. Part of the problem is that we are not sure how we feel about hell. Two little children were discussing Sunday school. One said, "We learned about the devil today, and he is awful." The other answered, "Oh, you don't have to worry. The devil is only make-believe; you know, like Santa Claus — he's really your father."

Some might agree with that, but not the early church. Not only did they believe in a real devil, they believed in the terrors of a real hell. They were desirous of avoiding it at all cost. A sermon from the 1740s shows that the concept of hell was used to scare people into heaven. Jonathan Edwards preached a sermon titled, "Sinners in the Hands of an Angry God." He depicted the sinner as being held over the yawning chasm of hell to roast in its flames eternally.

Today the fires of hell have been reduced to a pleasant glow, to the point where fear of it has little value, even as an inducement to be good. Yet the early church thought it was worth mentioning that Christ actually descended into hell. To them it showed that Christ had overcome every power of Satan. They believed that Christ went and preached salvation to all those departed spirits who had gone before him. Above all, it showed that no matter where people are, they are not beyond the power of Jesus to save. But it became so difficult to understand or to explain why a good man would go to hell, that some denominations changed it to say, "He went to the place of departed spirits." Others, like the Methodists, have simply reduced it to a footnote.

What happened to Jesus during that interval between his death and resurrection is not described by him, but if he experienced death as we are taught, then undoubtedly, he went to wherever it is that the dead go. And in that abode of departed spirits he may well have proclaimed the gospel of God's love to those who had not heard it. But that is not the topic I wish to deal with today.

Throughout the history of the church people have been attempting to make the elements of Jesus' life relevant to the people of their time. This is as it should be, but sometimes ideas and metaphors relevant to one era become stumbling blocks to people of another era. Therefore, in every generation people should struggle to place Christian truths in thought forms relevant to the day, and to be liberated from concepts of the past which no longer have meaning.

Instead of saying, "He descended into hell," I think it would be more meaningful to us to say "Jesus went through hell for us." When he entered Jerusalem on that first Palm Sunday to the accompaniment of shouted praise, he was taking the first step into the hell of suffering and death that was to follow. It is to the significance of that suffering and death, referred to in the Apostles' Creed, that I would now like to turn.

In theology, explanations of the death of Christ are called theories of the atonement, and there are many. Some of them go back to an ancient world where, in every land, the altars ran red with the blood of sacrifices, sometimes animal, sometimes human. Somehow, around those reeking altars, which would nauseate us, primitive people felt that their relationship with the unseen world of spirits was made secure. The ancient Germans, for example, in time of famine, first slew animals before the altar. If no relief came, humans were sacrificed. If there was still no relief, the chieftain himself gave up his life. Our Anglo-Saxon forebears also felt that without the shedding of blood there was no blessing. Consequently, our English words "bless" and "blood" come from the same stem.

In Judaism the system of animal sacrifices in the temple ritual was quite elaborate, and its description takes up considerable space in the Old Testament. It is no wonder, therefore, that Paul, brought up under that system, would exclaim, "Christ, our Passover lamb, has been sacrificed" (1 Corinthians 5:7). Similarly, the author of the book of Hebrews, looking for ways to tie Christianity to Judaism, says of Christ, "He entered once for all into the holy place, taking not the blood of goats and calves, but his own blood" (Hebrews 9:12).

Today, much Christian theology is still based on that analogy of blood sacrifice. People say that Jesus has saved them from sin. When one asks, "How?" They say, "By shedding his blood on the cross." When one asks what that accomplished, they say, "He died in order to make God's forgiveness possible." If one proceeds to question any further, he may be told that it is all a mystery, and that the person explaining it doesn't understand either. Some of our familiar hymns perpetuate ideas that are either obsolete or misleading. For example these words:

> *There is a Fountain, filled with blood,*
> *Drawn from Emmanuel's veins,*
> *And sinners plunged beneath its flood*
> *Lose all their guilty stains.*
> (William Cowper, 1771, "There Is A Fountain")

Surely, there must be a way of describing the death of Christ which is more meaningfully related to our own experience than that of bloody sacrifice.

Some theories about the meaning of the death of Christ are based on rather inadequate impressions of God. In the eleventh century a theologian by the name of Anselm taught that God was to be seen as a great feudal lord. Every person owed God perfect obedience. For a person to sin was to defraud God of his due and thereby acquire infinite guilt. Infinite guilt required infinite punishment: a person's eternal doom in hell. The only way out was for the infinite price to be paid by someone who is both God and man. Christ paid the price by his death on the cross. A ransom was paid to God for our redemption.

Try fitting that with Jesus' parable of the prodigal son. The prodigal has sinned against his father, and the father sees the returning son, penitent and ashamed, coming home from the far country. Instead of running and falling on the prodigal's neck, however, the father has to wait for a legal reparation to be made. There must be an elder brother who will volunteer to let himself be flogged to death, crucified, or whatever, so that the father's legal honor can be satisfied. Only then can the father welcome his son. That is not the way Jesus told the story — and I think Jesus' version is closer to the truth.

I acknowledge that Jesus died. I acknowledge that he died for me; but I do not think it is necessary to say that God demanded Jesus' death so that I could be forgiven. That doesn't square with a loving father.

The third thing I would like to do in this message is to offer an understanding of the suffering and death of Christ — his going through hell for us — which, I think, is meaningful for our time. It involves the idea of vicarious sacrifice, which means that someone who doesn't have to do it, voluntarily takes on the burdens of others. Some years ago, when I was in training for the Army chaplaincy, I was stationed at Fort Slocum, New York. On that base there was a chapel named Chapel of the Four Chaplains. In the chapel was a large stained-glass window that depicted the deck of a sinking troop transport during World War II. The ship had been torpedoed and as many of the soldiers came up on deck, they neglected to bring their life preservers with them. Each of the chaplains had worn a life preserver but had given it up to a serviceman who was without one. They went down with the ship to save others.

That is a concept we can understand in our day, because it's not related to outmoded animal sacrifice or legalistic formulae. We have as much right to think of Christ's death in terms understandable and reasonable in our time as people like Anselm had in their time.

Christ's death was a part of his life. His life and death were based on dedicated self-sacrifice for the good of others. In the book titled *Through the Valley of the Kwai*, a British officer describes the hardships and privation endured by himself and his men when they were prisoners of war at a Japanese prison camp in Southeast Asia during World War II. The prisoners were used by their Japanese taskmasters to build a railroad. On one occasion, as the work detail was coming to a close for the day, the Japanese soldiers came up to the group and excitedly indicated that a shovel was missing, and unless the person who had lost it confessed, all would be killed. The guards then began to beat the prisoners, and it was evident that they would carry out their threat. At that point one of the men stepped forward and confessed that he had lost the shovel. He was then brutally beaten to death. When the work detail came back to the prison compound and put away their tools, all the shovels were accounted for. Someone bore the burden in order to save the others.

Christ had a message that God loves and accepts all people. He tried to act that out, so that people could see what a life controlled by love would be like. Such a life made people uncomfortable because it seemed to be a judgment upon them; it called for changes they were unwilling to make; it disturbed the way things were; so people became hostile. All Jesus had to do was to back off, keep the message to himself, and he could have disappeared into oblivion without being hurt. But love for wayward people so filled his life that he was determined to give expression to that love, even if the forces hostile to him should take his life. Therefore, he died as he lived — a savior, saving people from wasted, futile, meaningless lives of self-centeredness. That's what it means to me when I say that Jesus is my savior: He gave his life willingly, not to make it possible for God to love me, but he gave his life proclaiming that God has always loved me. God did not demand Jesus' death, but God permitted his death in order that I might get the message. For if Jesus had not died that way, I probably never would have heard of him or of God's love either.

The salvation that Jesus proclaimed is certainly unique in its scope and impact, but the principle of vicarious sacrifice is not reserved for him alone. Wherever there is salvation in this world from any evil, there is vicarious sacrifice. Someone who doesn't have to volunteers to shoulder the burden of another: the healthy for the sick; the educated for the ignorant; the privileged for the underprivileged; the innocent for the guilty. In his book, *A Tale of Two Cities*, Charles Dickens tells the story of Charles Darney, who has been imprisoned and condemned to death during the French Revolution. His friend, Sidney Carten, has done everything he can to secure the release of Darney. When it appears there is no other way to save the prisoner, Sidney Carten and a friend go to visit Darney in his prison cell. There they drug the weakened prisoner. The friend then takes the drugged Darney from the prison cell and Sidney Carten is executed in his place. Someone who did not have to volunteer to take the burden of another.

The work of salvation is something in which all of us share. When Walt Whitman was working among the wounded during our Civil War, he wrote, "I do not ask the wounded person how he feels, I myself become the wounded person." He took on the burdens of others. Too often, theories of the atonement assume that by one single high-priestly act of self-sacrifice Christ saved the world. When Christ passed around the cup he said, "All of you, drink from it. Christ's life of saviorhood is to be continued in the vicarious sacrifice of his disciples.

On that day so long ago when Jesus entered the city of Jerusalem, he was beginning his descent into hell on our behalf. He was taking on a burden he did not need to bear in order to bring about our salvation, and he calls us to do the same for others.

In Graham Greene's novel *The Power and the Glory*, he tells the story of a priest in Mexico during the period when priests were being severely persecuted. The goal was to destroy the church. Priests were hunted and shot by the military with only the pretense of a trial. The priest fears for his life, yet he is aware that in the celebration of the mass and in his words of absolution, the grace of God comes to brow-beaten peasants. Some foreigners befriend the priest in a mountain village and make arrangements for him to go just a three days journey to the village of Las Casas where he will be safe. As soon as he has finished his sacramental duties, in the early morning hours, he prepares to leave. At that moment a message comes from a hardened criminal who is dying and is four or five hours in the opposite direction. That is where the police who have vowed to get the priest are waiting. The criminal has scribbled a note: "For Christ's sake, father, please come." The priest knows that the police will be waiting for him. He knows there is safety in Las Casas. But the criminal is dying, and the priest believes that his presence is needed to hear the man's confession, to grant him absolution, and to administer the last rites so that the criminal may spend eternity in God's presence. The priest feels he has no choice. His place is by the side of the dying man. It is there that the power and the glory of the gospel are discovered.

Whenever there is salvation in this world, whether it is from ignorance, disease, poverty, or hatred, it comes about because someone who doesn't have to goes through hell for someone else. There are so many places where salvation still needs to be brought, and those of us who follow Jesus are called upon to do the bringing.

MAUNDY THURSDAY

Something New
John 13:34

So much about the Christian calendar eludes us. We have words like Pentecost and Epiphany that are used only in church. If someone were to ask us what these words mean, we would probably answer, "I don't know. It's Greek to me." And in so answering, we would be quite right. The words are not understood by us because they *are* Greek.

Some words don't make sense because they are corruptions of our own language. For example, we might ask, "What is good about Good Friday?" It seems to us that it should have been called "Bad Friday."

But the name doesn't come from our word "Good" it comes from the word "God" so that its meaning is "God's Friday." In a similar way, we have contracted a blessing, "God be with you" into the more familiar "Good-bye."

Still other words come to us from Latin, and so are seldom used outside the church. Words like "Lent" and "Advent." And there is the word that brings us together this evening: Maundy-Thursday. The first time people hear the term they are apt to think that it is some peculiar juggling of the calendar, to make a day called "Monday-Thursday." "Maundy" comes from the Latin word *mondatum* meaning "commandment." It refers to a statement made by Jesus in which he says, "A new commandment I give you, that you love one another, even as I have loved you, that you also love one another." John tells us that these words were uttered in the context of the last meal Jesus shared with his disciples before his crucifixion. As we have gathered here this evening to participate in that last supper, it is appropriate that we spend a few minutes considering that new commandment, the one that makes this "Maundy-Thursday."

The first thing I want to say is that the *essence* of this commandment is not new. The Old Testament Jews knew about it. In Leviticus 19 it is written: "You shall love your neighbor as yourself." The problem was that the commandment had become narrowly defined. "Neighbor" had come to mean "Jew" and beyond that it had come to mean "only the Jew who is near to you." The Jews, who believed that they had experienced the love of God, did not acknowledge that that love was for *all* people. By the time of Jesus, the commandment had been corrupted to read: "You shall love your *friends* and hate your *enemies*."

The Gentiles also were aware of love. In fact, they had many words for it. The Greeks had the word *phileo*, from which we get the idea of filial or brotherly love. They had the word *eros*, from which we get the idea of erotic or romantic love. There was *agape*, a little-used form of self-giving love or good will, much used by Christian writers. Unfortunately, even though the Gentiles had this word in their vocabulary, they didn't distribute their love very widely.

We have some experience with love, too, even apart from a Christian understanding. Most of us have experienced love in the family — something that we feel for close relations and something they feel for us — fondness, affection, obligation — this is what we mean when we say, "Blood is thicker than water." We also use the word in a sexual sense, as when we speak of "making love" — a term which has become so corrupted that it has little to do with real love, but only satisfaction. We use the word to describe romantic attraction, as when we say we are "in love"! We speak of "loving" other people in the sense that we have a high regard for them. Perhaps that is what we mean when we speak of loyalty or dedication. All these things we can experience quite apart from anything we have learned from Christ. Whatever Jesus meant by calling this a new commandment, it was not new in the sense of not having been known before.

The second thing I would like to point out is that though the essence of love was not new, the *example* that Jesus offered was new: "Love one another as I have loved you." This is not love that is based on feelings of affection for the recipient. We can't be commanded to *feel* something toward another person, but we can be required to *act* in certain ways. This "love" of which Jesus speaks is an attitude — an attitude that culminates in action. It is most especially illustrated by doing something for someone that they cannot do for themselves. The good Samaritan didn't have to like the fellow he helped, but he became an example of love by doing the humane, the just, the compassionate thing. In this congregation, we provide shelter for homeless people, not because we feel regard for or closeness to the people we help but because at the moment they need help, and we take our lesson in love from Jesus, who had compassion on the people among whom he walked.

By his example, Jesus also indicates that our expressions of love are not dependent upon the worthiness of the recipient either. In the night in which Jesus spoke of his love for his followers, Judas, who later betrayed him, was present. Peter, who out of fear later denied him, was there. Thomas, who was always pessimistic, and whose faith wavered, was there. Paul, who earlier persecuted the church, testified that he had experienced Christ's love. Typically, we love those who are worthy of our love and are in a position to return it, because for us, love is dependent upon feelings of affection. The love inspired by Christ, however, causes us to do right by a person, not because the person is worthy of our effort, but because the person is a child of God.

Because of the context in which these words are found, we cannot overlook the lesson that the kind of love Jesus is speaking about is love that is shown by service. Jesus took a bowl and a towel and washed his disciples' feet. "This is what I mean by love," he was saying. People who love submit themselves in service. It wasn't a compassionate act in the sense that life and limb depended on it. Rather, it was a way of showing that the one who loves must be ready to serve.

If love is to be useful, it can't be concerned about status. Most of us probably have fantasies about rendering some great social service. In our mind's eye, we see ourselves being publicly congratulated for some selfless thing that we have done. And certainly, if the level of praise were high enough, there are probably very few costly services that we would not render. But what Jesus was demonstrating was *menial* service that few, if any, would even notice. Yet, if Jesus, whom we call Lord and Savior, can do this small service with dignity, who are we to say that some worthwhile service is beneath us because no one will think of it as significant. It is his *example* of love that is new, and it is refreshing.

Not only do we see in Jesus an example of love, we also see something of its extent. Jesus left that upper room and went out to a cross. At the beginning of this passage, John says of Jesus that "having loved his own... he loved them to the end" (John 13:1). But "his own" were not simply those who loved him in return, or those who were obedient or worthy. "God so loved the world," John says, "that he sent his only begotten son, that whosoever believes in him, should not perish" (John 3:16). "God shows his love for us," says Paul, "in that, while we were still sinners, Christ died for us" (Romans 5:8). That sounds very noble and pious. It is the kind of thing we might expect God to do, but what has that to do with us? "Love one another... as *I* have loved *you*," said Jesus (John 13:34). That's what it has to do with us.

In one of his books Keith Miller tries to describe what he thinks is meant by Christian love. Sitting in his study, he could see his daughter riding her tricycle in the front driveway of his home. Far away he heard the squealing brakes of a garbage truck. In his mind's eye he saw his daughter go whizzing down the driveway and into the street in the path of that truck. He could see himself spring from his seat and rush to push the child out of the way, even though he knew the truck would crush him. He thought to himself, "That is love." Then he thought of the mean little kid with a runny nose, who called him names and threw rocks at his car. He saw that child rushing into the path of the truck, and again he saw himself springing to push that child out of the way too, while the truck rolled over his body. It occurred to him that *that* is *Christian* love: love that costs something to give.

This passage calls us to demonstrate a kind of love that is not sentimental, romantic, self-satisfying, or tied to the lovableness of the recipient. We are given a new commandment to love as Christ loved, which is what we do when we render service whether great or small.

GOOD FRIDAY

It Is Finished
John 19:30

When a football team wins a bowl game it has become customary to douse the winning coach with a container of ice water. It means that they have finished the season as champions. When a doctoral candidate completes his or her thesis there is a sense of fulfillment and the cry, "It's finished!" When a soldier at some forward observation point radios back to his command post and says, "We are finished," it has a different and ominous meaning.

When Jesus said from the cross, "It is finished," what did that mean? Was he saying, "I'm through. I've gone my limit and I have nothing to show for it but shame and defeat and death"? There certainly were those who must have heard it that way. The Roman soldiers might have dusted their hands and said "That's that." The Jewish authorities no doubt felt that it was "curtains" for this upstart. Even the disciples must have interpreted it as the end of a fine story.

One wonders how Jesus said it. Was it with a sense of relief that the suffering was drawing to a close? Was it with a sense of disappointment over what might have been? Was it with an attitude of resignation that the plan had failed? Or was it perhaps with a tone of exaltation that somehow this accomplished a certain goal? What do these words mean?

Well, for one thing, they certainly meant that his earthly life was finished. From the earliest days of the church Jesus' death has been difficult to explain. Around the year 300 AD, Arnobius, a pagan, wrote about the Christians, "We are not angry with you because you worship the omnipotent God, but because you pay daily homage to a man... who was put to death in a way that is a disgrace even to the vile."

It should be pointed out that the crucifixion of Jesus is an entirely unique event in the history of religion. No other founder of a great religion died a violent and voluntary death of self-sacrifice. Gotoma Buddha was past eighty when he died, surrounded by his faithful followers. Confucius passed away in peace at more than seventy years of age, serene and revered. Moses died at a ripe old age, foreseeing the conquest of the holy land. Mohammed, reclining on the breast of his wife, Ayesha, died when over sixty years of age, revered and victorious. Jesus, however, was executed on a cross, among criminals. He died after a brief ministry, still in his early thirties. He was betrayed, deserted, outcast, and mourned by few. Yet he seemed to have deliberately chosen the course of action that led to his crucifixion.

No wonder the church has attempted to explain his death. And the explanations have been many and varied taking into consideration the experiences of the audience. One explanation that seemed to make sense to the early Jewish Christians, who were acquainted with sacrifice, was that God's righteous wrath could be satisfied only by the supreme sacrifice of his own son, who was designated as the Lamb of God. Present-day Christians give expression to that understanding when they sing that hymn which says: "There is a fountain filled with blood, drawn from Emmanuel's veins, And sinners plunged beneath its flood, loose all their guilty stains." But this does not seem to square fully with Jesus' story of the prodigal son, who was received by the waiting father with no suggestion of wrath to be assuaged.

In the eleventh century Anselm taught that people's sins demanded eternal doom in hell. There must be either punishment or satisfaction. Jesus, he taught, took the punishment to satisfy God's justice. But we cannot help noting that if God is just, he is at least as just as humans, and people in the secular courts today would not consider it justice to have the innocent pay while the guilty go free. Early church leaders used the thought forms of their day to explain the crucifixion of Jesus in ways that their contemporaries would understand.

In a similar way, it is appropriate that we in our time should look for ways to explain the death of Christ in terms that are intelligible to us. And this we shall attempt to do. But let us agree that when Jesus said, "It is finished," he certainly was referring to his earthly life.

The second thing I think he meant is that his mission had been accomplished. All through life he had been aware of a mission. As a youth of twelve he felt that God had a job for him to do. He said, "Did you not know that I must be about my Father's business?" (Luke 2:49). On other occasions he said, "We must work the works of him who sent me while it is yet day, for the night is coming when no one can work" (John 9:4). In Gethsemane, on the night before his death, he said in prayer, "I have finished the work you gave me to do" (John 17:4). The words "it is finished" certainly meant "mission accomplished."

And what was that mission? For one thing, his mission was to reveal what God is like. People had a number of unclear notions about God. Job, on his ash heap, thought of God as a hostile judge. Job felt that if only he could get a spokesman, someone to plead his case, he could turn away God's wrath and persuade God to accept him. Some systems of government have the office of Ombudsman, a spokesman who can go right to the top on behalf of a citizen. Job's conception of God was such that he felt that was what he needed; an Ombudsman. Other ancient Israelites thought more in terms of placating God's wrath with sacrifices of animals. Later, the prophets provided a corrective to this, pointing out that the sacrifices God really seeks are justice, mercy, humility, and repentance. But the basic assumption was still that God is essentially hostile toward the human race.

I think that assumption continues today in the minds of many people. When I was quite young, I delighted in playing with matches. Of all the places I could have chosen, I sat in a wood bin in the basement of our house to light the matches! Twice I set the bin on fire! In an effort to break me of this my mother took me to a local fire station where a firefighter took my name and talked sternly to me about how bad it was for little boys to play with matches. For years thereafter I avoided firefighters and fire trucks. When I came to a fire station I would cross the street to avoid passing it. I was sure they had my name and were looking for me. I never felt comfortable when Dick and Jane readers spoke of "our friends" at the fire station. It was nothing that firefighters had against me. It was my guilt that made me avoid them. I think that many of us, feeling guilty about one thing or another, sense a gulf between ourselves and God. The sense of alienation is real enough, but its foundation is in us, not in God.

Jesus' mission was to go beyond our assumptions of God's hostility and to reveal God as a God of love. He wanted people to understand that God is on our side. He loves the just and the unjust, the repentant and the unrepentant. Jesus taught it by parable. God is a waiting father, longing for the return of his erring child, whom he will gladly receive. More than that, God not only freely receives the sinner who turns to him in repentance, but God goes out in quest of the sinner who has not repented, as a shepherd goes out into the wilderness to find the one lost sheep.

Jesus also taught this by his life. He said, "The son of man has come to seek out and to save that which was lost" (Luke 19:10). Then he sat down with sinners and outcasts. In fact, he seemed to seek out *their* company in preference to that of the righteous. "No one has seen the Father at anytime," he said, "but the one who has seen me, has seen the Father" (John 14:9). Jesus' mission was to demonstrate God's acceptance of people. People felt that God had to be made to love them. John said, "God is love" (1 John 4:8). God now loves and always has loved the world.

In the early centuries those who were bishops of the church at Rome cast about for a high-sounding title that would describe their new, exalted position. They came upon the title "Pontifex Maximus." We still hear it today when the Pope is called "Supreme Pontiff." A pontiff is a bridge-builder. A Supreme Pontiff is the greatest bridge builder. It was a title taken from the Roman empire, a title for Caesar. But more than that, it described the mighty bridging which was accomplished when Jesus cried, "It is finished." His mission was to restore the relationship between God and humanity, which humans had broken by assuming a hostility in God which was never there. When he said, "It is finished," he meant "mission accomplished."

A third thing these words say to me is that Jesus was also finishing something in our behalf. This is called the "atonement." We have already indicated that by his life Jesus attempted to reconcile people with God. It was his intention to break down our defensive hostility by pointing out that God is *for* us, not *against* us. This is why some people have broken the word "atonement" into its components and described Jesus' life as one of "at-one-ment" — bringing God and humanity together. This describes the mission of his life, but we still have to put into modern terms an understanding of his death.

His death, too, was a part of the atonement, not to placate an angry God, but because in the nature of things, salvation involves sacrifice by one person for another. It is so in many fields. Salvation from the evils which plague our race come about when someone who does not have to takes on the burdens of others who may not even deserve that help. Researchers take on the burdens of the sick, and it leads to salvation from disease. Teachers take on the burdens of the unlearned, and it leads to salvation from ignorance. Doctors take on the burden of the injured, and we have salvation from death.

During the Vietnam War a missionary orphanage was bombed, killing several children and wounding several more. The townspeople appealed to the American forces for help, and a U.S. Navy doctor and nurse soon arrived at the bombed-out orphanage in a jeep. One patient, a young girl, needed an immediate blood transfusion, but neither of the Americans had the right type of blood. The American doctor knew just a little bit of Vietnamese and asked for a blood donor from among the children, explaining that without it the girl would die. A young boy named Heng nodded that he would be a donor. He was found to have the right blood type and he was prepared for the transfusion. He lay down on a table, extremely stiff and totally silent. As the nurse drew the blood, Heng burst into tears. This happened several times and the nurse could not console him. Eventually, a Vietnamese nurse showed up, saw how tense Heng was, and spoke to him in Vietnamese. Suddenly, the boy smiled and looked greatly relieved. The doctor asked the Vietnamese nurse what was going on and she explained that the boy thought that he was dying. He misunderstood the Americans' broken Vietnamese and thought that by giving his blood to the little girl, he would give up his life in exchange. They had the nurse ask him why, if he thought he would die, he offered to make the donation in the first place. "Because she is my friend." he answered.

Jesus did not hesitate to show himself as "the sinners' friend." He alienated the religious leaders by his habit of associating with men and women of doubtful character and by his acceptance of them. He seemed to be subverting all the rules of conduct by putting together the good and the bad, and teaching that all of us are equally dependent upon the grace of God. That is what got him into trouble with the leaders of his people. He would not be turned aside by their opposition, for what they so disliked was the very thing he knew he had to do. He continued to be the friend of sinners, offering forgiveness and salvation, and he got deeper and deeper into trouble, until in the end, he was condemned to death. He took our burdens when he did not have to in order to demonstrate the lengths to which God would go to call us to our senses. This is the reason why the New Testament says that Christ died: "The righteous for the unrighteous, that he might bring us to God." It was this that he was finishing on the cross.

Centuries ago the inhabitants of Taiwan were known for the wide-spread practice of headhunting. The practice was brought to an end largely through the work of a benevolent Chinese magistrate by the name of Gaw Hong, who, by his kind and just dealings with the tribesmen, gained their love and respect. Steadily, he worked to stamp out the old blood-feuds and headhunting. But a great religious feast was approaching and the tribesmen became troubled because they believed that the gods demanded human heads. They went to Gaw Hong and pleaded for permission to placate their deity in the time-honored manner. The magistrate reasoned with them, tried to postpone a decision, pointed out that old feuds would begin again, but finally, worn down by their importunity, he consented. "Take one head." he said. "Only one. And take it when, and where I tell you." When the day of the feast was at hand, Gaw Hong told them what to do. They were to take the head of the first man coming down a certain path in a certain wood at dawn the next day. The next morning in the gray light of dawn, a man came down the path. The arrow found its mark, the head was quickly severed and put in a sack. When the waiting chiefs opened the sack, there was the head of Gaw Hong. That day, the tribal chiefs took a vow never again to take a head, and that barbarity was brought to an end through the sacrifice of one person.

Vicarious sacrifice: someone who does not have to giving his sacrificial all for the benefit of others. That ingredient is surely at the heart of what Jesus was finishing for us on the cross.

Perhaps no one explanation can deal adequately with that mystery, but there is a hymn I think expresses for us feelings which no amount of theology can adequately describe:

> *When I survey the wondrous cross*
> *On which the Prince of Glory died,*
> *My richest gain I count but loss,*
> *And pour contempt on all my pride.*
> *Were the whole realm of nature mine,*
> *That were an offering far too small;*
> *Love so amazing, so divine,*
> *Demands my soul, my life, my all.*
> (Isaac Watts, 1707, "When I Survey The Wondrous Cross")

EASTER SUNDAY

Point Me Toward Tomorrow
Mark 16:1-8

Ben Haden tells the story of a group of four year olds who were gathered in a Sunday school class in Chattanooga. The teacher looked at the class and asked: "What special day was last Sunday?" A little four-year-old girl held up her hand and said, "Last Sunday was Palm Sunday." The teacher exclaimed, "That's fantastic, that's wonderful. Now, does anyone know what today is called?" The same little girl held up her hand and said, "Yes, today is Easter Sunday." Once again the teacher said, "That's fantastic. Now, does anyone know why we celebrate Easter?" The same little girl responded and said, "We celebrate Easter because Jesus rose from the grave," and before the teacher could congratulate her, she kept on talking and said, "but if he sees his shadow... he has to go back in for seven weeks."

It's not easy to keep the Easter story straight, especially when so many other things get attached to it. So today I'd like for us to go over the story once more, not only to pick up some of the details, but to see what the resurrection of Jesus means for our lives.

In the gospel according to Mark, we heard how three women came to a grave to do what people have traditionally done for the dead, but they couldn't even find the body. Instead, they heard the words, "He has risen. He is not here." Truly, something significant had happened to Jesus, but what is the message this event has for us?

The first thing this Easter narrative says to me is that life is filled with temptations to hold on to the past. When those women came to the tomb, it was out of respect for a remembered life. There had been no time to render the last service to the body of Jesus. The sabbath had intervened, and the women, who wished to anoint the body, had not been able to do so. Now the sabbath had passed, and as early as possible, they set out to accomplish their sad task. They had heard

Jesus preach and teach, they had witnessed his acts of compassion, they had thought that he was to become the Messiah. Then they had witnessed his cruel death and burial. Their minds were occupied with thoughts of what might have been. As long as their attention was focused on the past, their gloom was unrelieved.

Hasn't that been our experience too? When we lose someone we love, we are frequently led to the place where we can be close to the body that housed that spirit. We may make visits to the grave. No doubt that is a normal part of grief. But on those occasions, we are tempted to reflect on the past, and if we are not careful, we may make the past the center of everything that is important.

Aristotle Onassis began his incredible career as a seventeen-year-old refugee with only $100 in his pocket. At the pinnacle of his power in 1973, his estimated worth was more than one billion dollars. His philosophy was captured in one succinct statement: "All that really counts these days is money. It's the people with money who are the royalty now." In 1973, his 24-year-old son, Alexander, was killed in a plane crash, and the world of Aristotle Onassis began to crumble. Onassis was unable to cope with his grief. *Time* magazine quoted one associate as saying, "He aged overnight. He suddenly became an old man. In business negotiations, he was uncharacteristically absentminded, irrational, and petulant." Within one year, his fortune declined from one billion to half that, and not long after, Aristotle Onassis himself died. Grief can cause us to live in the past.

Guilt, too, can tie us to the past. In San Jose, California, there is a house that was built over a 38-year period at a cost of five million dollars. The 160-room house has stairways that lead to blank walls, corridors that lead to unopenable doors, thirteen bathrooms, thirteen stair steps, thirteen lights to a chandelier, thirteen windows to a room. The house, built by the widow of William Wirt Winchester, son of the manufacturer of the Winchester repeating rifle, is also referred to as a "guilt house." A spiritualist in Boston told Mrs. Winchester that if she were to move West and start a never-ending building project, she could provide a home for the spirits of those killed by Winchester rifles and assuage her own guilt over those deaths. Her method of dealing with guilt gave her no rest. Instead of facing it and leaving it in the past, it occupied her whole life.

Fear is another thing that can keep us in the past. Thomas Noton tells of a woman who writes romance novels. She's written twelve novels. If each were exactly 65,000 words, that would be a total of 780,000 words. Each novel has all the basic elements of fine fiction. This lady has gone to the trouble of creating a minor city with an ocean-front location. She creates common landmarks that are visual in each novel, linking one novel to the next like a running soap opera. Yet this woman has never had a book published. A single rejection slip so devastated her that she quit sending her work out. She dreams about being published. She continues to write. She's working on another novel, set in the same beautiful city-by-the-sea, with characters that walk off the pages, and scenes that intimately involve the reader. But she has no plans to send this one out either. She is imprisoned by fear of rejection.

Still others want to hold on to the past because they are afraid of dying themselves. Charles Platt, in an article titled "Silicon Man," tells of his decision to have his body preserved. "So far, in the United States, perhaps one person in a million has made financial arrangements to be frozen after death. And I am one of those people — a crackpot or a visionary, depending on your point of view. I have contracted to store my remains in liquid nitrogen. Two or three centuries in the future, when medical science is sufficiently advanced, I hope to be brought back to life." He tells how he became impressed with the possibility of preserving the body by visiting Alcor, a cryonics organization in Riverside, California. He then continues: "Cryonics isn't cheap, and Alcor's current minimum fee of $41,000 is out of reach for most of us. The fee can be covered by a life insurance policy that makes Alcor the beneficiary. To me, this money wasn't trivial. But facing my own mortality turned out to be much harder than coming up with the cash to pay $450 a year for the life insurance premiums and the annual Alcor membership fee." The fear of dying can cause many people to hold on to what is familiar — even a worn-out body — rather than to embrace their future. Like those women coming to the tomb, we are tempted to hold on to the past, but the past is not where we find life.

The second thing this passage suggests to me is that God helps us in the present. Those women, heading for the tomb on that Easter morning, became aware that they had a problem: There was a large circular stone covering the mouth of the tomb. It would be too big for them to push aside. They were confronted with their own helplessness. Then they discovered, upon arrival, that the stone had been rolled away; the obstacle had been removed. More than that; the grave was empty! And there was someone there to tell them what had happened. What they could not do had been done for them.

I would submit that God provides help for us in dealing with our present problems. There are some things that are beyond our ability to deal with unaided. They are bigger than we are, and if we don't get help they will destroy us.

For example, consider guilt, which we mentioned earlier. Tom Anderson knew about guilt. As a young man he was involved in a foolish college fraternity hazing incident that resulted in the death of a fellow student. The horror of that episode stayed with Tom for many years. He couldn't shake it. His guilt ruined him professionally and cost him his marriage. Then, one day, something happened that changed his life. Listen to how he tells it: "I used to think, 'Nothing can undo what I have done.' The thought of my guilt would stop me in the middle of a smile or a handshake. It put a wall between my wife and me. Then I had an unexpected visit from the person I most dreaded to see — the mother of the college classmate who died. 'Years ago,' she said, 'I found it in my heart, through prayer, to forgive you. So have your wife, your friends, and employers.' She paused, and then said sternly, 'You are the only person who hasn't forgiven Tom Anderson. Who do you think you are to stand out against the people of the town and the Lord almighty?' I looked into her eyes and found there a kind of permission to be the person I might have been if her boy had lived. For the first time in my adult life I felt worthy to love and be loved." Tom Anderson went on to become a successful businessman. He and his wife put their marriage back together again. God used a grieving mother to give Tom Anderson back his life.

God also uses people to redeem *us* from failure. A highly touted 22-year-old stood alone on the vast La Scala Opera stage. This was his big moment to audition for the impresario, *Despuro*. The music started and the young man stood stunned and unresponsive. Belatedly, he made a few awkward gestures and equally improper sounds. Then he became silent and dizzy. He had lost control of his mind, voice, and body. At that moment, the young man began to tremble and weep. Offstage a moment later, the mortified youth vowed never to sing again. His wise teacher said, "No, no, little one. We will make our climb more slowly. And some day, some day, La Scala will come to us." Fortunately for the music world, Enrico Caruso had a teacher who could provide the encouragement he could not give himself.

God can use the strangest experiences to relieve us of our fear of death too. Richard Wright tells how it happened for him. "When I was a boy I had a paper route in one of the poorest sections of town. I discovered that rather than go around the whole block, I could ride through the back alley and throw the papers to the houses on either side. Thus, I covered the area much quicker. There was one drawback. In the alley there was the biggest, fiercest old black Chow dog I had ever seen. We did battle every morning. I carried rocks, clubs, sprays, and anything else that would help me overcome my fear of his daily attack. Every day that Chow would come charging out at me, but I knew where he would come from and would be going fast and just lift my legs and coast out of harm's way. One dark morning I started through the alley with my papers and a club, but the enemy didn't appear. I relaxed, threw down my club, and was about to exit the alley when, at that precise moment, the hairy monster came roaring out from under the porch of the last possible house. Before I knew it, he had fastened his dreadful huge jaws on the smallest part of the calf of my leg. You can imagine my fear when he bit down with a powerful crunch. You cannot imagine my sense of relief and joyful laughter when I realized, for the first time in years, that the old Chow dog was harmless — he didn't have a tooth in his head.

From that day on that old back alley was a different place. It no longer held terror for me. I had been delivered from all my unfounded fears. When I think of Saint Paul's saying about death having no sting, I sometimes say to myself: 'One bright morning, God's people that have so feared death will look into its ugly jaws and shout — O death, where is your terror, O grave, where is your bite?' Thank God that on the first Easter morning, by delivering Jesus Christ from our final enemy, God has removed all the teeth and the terror of dying; and if we are wise, the terror of living as well."

God rolled away the stone on that Easter morning, not to let Jesus out, but to open the tomb for inspection. Death does not need to hold us in fear, for Christ has overcome death, and because he lives, we too shall live. That puts a new light on the present.

The third thing this Easter narrative says to me is that Jesus not only meets us in the present, he leads us into the future. The women at the tomb were met by a messenger who told them that Jesus was going before them into Galilee. Jesus was always like that, out in front, leading the way, his face set toward the future. That is why the author of the book of Hebrews calls him the pioneer of our faith; he was out on the frontiers.

At the southernmost point of South Africa is a cape round which the storms are always raging. For a thousand years no one knew what lay beyond that cape, for no ship had ever returned to tell the tale. It was called the Cape of Storms. In the sixteenth century a Portuguese explorer, Vasco da Gama, successfully sailed around the cape and found beyond it a great calm sea, and beyond that, the shores of India. So the name of the cape was changed to the Cape of Good Hope. Until that first Easter morning, death had been the cape of storms on which the hopes of all humankind were wrecked, and no one knew what lay beyond it. But now, in the light of Easter, it has become for all who believe in Christ the cape of good hope. He leads us through death.

By the resurrection of Jesus, God gives us a new way of looking at death. It is true that death temporarily closes the door on relationships here, but it opens the door to other relationships. Henry Van

Dyke, in *A Parable of Immortality*, reminds us of that opening door with another analogy taken from the sea. He wrote, "I am standing upon the seashore. A ship at my side spreads her white sails to the morning breeze and starts for the blue ocean. She is an object of beauty and strength, and I stand and watch until at last she hangs like a speck of white cloud just where the sea and sky come down to mingle with each other. Then someone at my side says, 'There, she's gone!' Gone where? Gone from my sight, that is all. She is just as large in mast and hull and spar as she was when she left my side, and just as able to bear her load of living freight to the place of destination. Her diminished size is in me, not in her. And just at the moment when someone at my side says, 'There, she's gone!' there are other eyes watching her coming and other voices ready to take up the glad shout, 'There, she's come!' " And that is dying.

In a film titled *I'll Sing, Not Cry*, a documentary about missionary work in Africa, a story is told about Pastor Ngonga, whose beloved wife has died. A large number of people came to the funeral. Following their tradition, they sat on the ground and began to wail, Christians and animists alike, blending their voices in the usual dirge of despair. Ngonga had loved his wife, but that day he stood beside her coffin and cried out in a commanding voice: "Stop all this yelling and howling!" The mourners stared at him in shocked silence. Then Ngonga spoke more quietly: "This woman," he said, "was a child of God. She has gone home to her Father. Today we are not going to cry; we are going to sing!" With that, he started to sing, and the shamefaced Christians joined in. It was not a song sung in fear of a departed spirit that rose in the air around the dead one, but a hymn of praise to God, a song of Christ's victory. They carried her body to its resting place to the accompaniment of songs.

When the women in our gospel reading for this morning headed out to the grave where Jesus was buried, it was with heavy hearts, because they were aware that Jesus had died. But when they arrived at the tomb, found the stone rolled away, discovered that the body was gone, and heard the testimony of the messenger: "He has risen, he is not here," they got the rest of the message: "Jesus is alive, and has gone on before you into Galilee. Go and tell his disciples." By his resurrection Jesus turns us from the past and points us toward tomorrow.

PENTECOST SUNDAY

The Tower and the Flame
Genesis 11:1-9; Acts 2:1-6

In the film *Mosquito Coast* an eccentric inventor decides to bring the benefits of civilization to primitive natives living in the interior of Central America. He concludes that the most significant creation of civilization is the ability to make ice. He settles his family in the jungle and proceeds to build an enormous ice-producing plant. He wraps his first product, a huge block of ice, in burlap and proceeds to drag it a few days' journey through the jungle to a primitive tribe. By the time he gets to the natives, the ice has melted and the natives are not impressed.

There are definite benefits to civilization and ice may be one of them. Civilization also provides us with transportation, rapid communication, entertainment, culture, and medical technology. But city life or urban civilization also has many problems. Robbery, assault, murder, crowding, civil strife, ghettos, taxation, and restrictive ordinances, all tend to make the values of living together a very mixed blessing.

The author of the Genesis story we read this morning did not consider civilization to be a blessing at all. He was no doubt influenced by the nomadic preferences of his ancestors, and felt that whenever people settled down in urban civilizations, bad things happened. In his estimation, urbanization and settled life had a bad history. He reported that the first founder of a city was Cain, who was the first murderer. When Noah became settled after the flood, he planted a vineyard, got drunk, and was involved in some debased sexual conduct. When people settled around Babylon, it led to disordered relationships among people and between people and God.

Many feel that civilized society has only gotten worse. Since we are obliged to live in modern civilization, we would do well to listen to what the authors of our scripture lessons have to say about it.

The first thing the author of the Genesis passage does is to give a little historical background on the development of civilization from his point of view. He says that people came from the East to the plain of Shinar. Shinar is lower Mesopotamia, the home of the ancient Sumerians. The Sumerians themselves wrote of a land of Dilmun in the East, from which they had come. Archeological discoveries indicate that it was indeed these people who established the first civilization.

The author says these people built a tower and a city and called it Babylon, coming from an Akkadian word meaning "Gate of the Gods." Here was an urban civilization complete with skyscrapers, and the evidence left behind corroborates the Genesis account. In fact, there were many towers on the Mesopotamian plain: 33 of them. They were called ziggurats, an Akkadian word meaning "to be high or raised up." Generally, the towers were a series of terraces with a shrine at the top. The tower of Babylon was reported to be seven stories high and rose to a height of 300 feet. It was named "The house of the foundation of heaven and earth," and it represented the high point of human striving toward civilization in those days.

The author was not much impressed by the accomplishments of this civilization, however. Many contemporary observers have a similar view. In a speech that he gave as vice president, Al Gore gave a similar assessment of contemporary civilization when he stated that: "We have constructed in our civilization a false world of plastic flowers and Astro-Turf, air conditioning and fluorescent lights, windows that don't open and background music that never stops, days when we don't know whether it has rained, nights when the sky never stops glowing, Walkman® and Watchman®, entertainment cocoons, frozen food for the microwave oven, sleepy hearts jump-started by caffeine, alcohol, drugs, and illusions." Civilization still has problems.

The second thing the author does is to list some of the reasons why civilized society has such problems. For one thing, he notes that the accomplishments of civilization tend to foster pride. "Let us make a name for ourselves," said these people. A primary root of trouble in human history is pride in our technological advancements, which keeps us from focusing on more basic areas. The pharaohs of Egypt, for example, built pyramids to assure their own immortality, because Egypt had the technical ability. Yet the very building of those pyramids served to perpetuate the injustice of slavery in Egypt, and thus accelerated the decay of a way of life that the pyramids were intended to preserve.

The conflict between pride of achievement and a fallen humanity is lifted up by J. Aller as he writes about an experience he had while visiting a strange city. "I was stuck in my hotel during a recent trip to Seattle," he writes. "Nothing is more boring than to be in a strange city as the visiting prophet.

"I had spoken all day at conferences, and here I was all alone. Seeking amusement, I flipped on the TV. There, live and direct, was the space shuttle crew. I must admit I marveled at man's technological successes. There they were, hundreds of miles up in space, tethered to their craft by a thin nylon line, walking in space. Walking in space! Who could imagine such a thing?

"Later, I passed by the front desk. The clerk asked if I needed a cab. 'No, I'm going jogging.' 'Well,' he warned, 'stay out of the park. You might get mugged.' I decided to jog to the coffee shop instead. As I sat there I gazed across the street and could see the park. I had a sad thought, 'We can walk in space, but we can't walk in our parks.'

"Such are the achievements of our race. Since the Tower of Babel we have supposed that we can work out our own salvation with technological advancement. The primary delusion of humankind is the belief that we will eventually create heaven on earth. Because of the fallen nature of the race, we can walk in space, but we can't walk in our parks."

Another problem associated with civilization noted by the author of the Genesis story is a tendency to lose contact with God. The people in our story said, "Let the top of our tower reach to heaven." They wanted a high tower to make them equal with God. It was the Garden of Eden all over again. When people think that they are equal with God, God becomes unnecessary.

In 1983, when Alexander Solzhenitsyn received the Templeton Award in London, he began his speech by saying, "Over half a century ago, while I was still a child, I recall hearing a number of older people offer the following explanation for the great disasters that had befallen Russia: (people) have forgotten God. That's why all this has happened! ... And if I were called upon to identify briefly the principal trait of the entire twentieth century, here too, I would be unable to find anything more precise and pithy than to repeat once again (people) have forgotten God."

His remarks are not simply a description of godless Russia. A *Newsweek* article asks: "When did you last reboot? In need of a little absolution? Dump your sins at the Confession Booth, a worldwide web program created by Ken Lang, a computer-science graduate student at Carnegie Mellon University. Once at the site, type in your sin(s). A digital priest will dole out a penance. Lang, who says he 'believes in some form of a god,' estimates that between 200 and 500 users drop to their knees each day. Strengthen your resolve at http://antherlearning.cs.cmu.edu/priest.html." A technological society can cause us to think that God is irrelevant to our needs.

Another problem for the people of our story was materialism. To them the erection of the tower was a most important consideration. Their goals had become increasingly materialistic.

Marshall Blonsky is a professor at New York University and an analyst of cultural change. He had this exchange with a reporter at Nike Town, a glittering new store on Michigan Avenue in Chicago that sells wildly expensive sneakers: "This," said Blonsky on entering the store, "is a church! A post-modern church!" Then pointing to a life-sized figure of Michael Jordan, the basketball star, he declared, "Look! There's God!" This was not just crude and blasphemous flippancy. He went on to explain that many people today are totally unpersuaded by any system of beliefs. For them, flashy shoes are as important as anything gets. Beyond a fascination with the ownership of impressive things, Blonsky cites as other key values of the New Culture glamour, fitness, youth, power, freedom, eroticism, and violence.

We are physical and spiritual beings. When our total focus is on material goals, we move away from our potential.

The author goes on to show that in a secular society, not only is the individual cut off from God, but from other people as well. We read that their language became confused, and they no longer understood each other. What actually happened is not known but the confusion of language is a very fitting symbol of the division, strangeness, suspicion, and hostility that has arisen among members of the human race.

Not speaking the same language leads to confusion. A foreign student was asked about the health of his convalescing wife. He replied, "She is not as painful as she was, but she is still very tiresome."

Not speaking the same language leads to misunderstanding. A Canadian tourist in a Madrid restaurant wanted to order steak and mushrooms. He spoke no Spanish and the waiter spoke no English. The Canadian, in an attempt to communicate, drew a picture of a cow and a mushroom on the menu and handed it to the waiter. The waiter returned a few minutes later with an umbrella and a ticket to the bullfights.

Not speaking the same language leads to isolation. I am acquainted with another fellow who traveled to Europe on his own and found the language barrier so difficult for him that he purchased canned foods and ate many of his meals uncooked in his room, which is not the way to enjoy Europe!

The gist of the whole story of Babel is to point up the futility, the emptiness, the loneliness that is experienced by human beings when they have displaced God and become insensitive to one another.

Fortunately, that is not where the biblical narrative ends. If Babel speaks of the problems of civilization, the second story we read this morning — the story of Pentecost in the book of Acts — speaks of the solution. Babel describes humanity's daily experience of separation from God and one another; Pentecost describes the possibility of reunion. Consider what happened. Fifty days following the resurrection of Christ, a small group of timid Christian disciples were together in one place. They had nothing in common except devotion to a common Lord: They had experienced Jesus Christ. Suddenly, they became aware of a mysterious presence that filled them and took away their timidity. So over-powering was this common experience that they ran into the city to share it. So infectious was their enthusiasm — so passionate their conviction — that they conveyed the power of their message even to those who did not understand their language. People from varying backgrounds heard them and understood. So basic was their message to the needs of all people that Luke describes the disciples as being able to speak the languages of all present. The confusion brought about by human pride, materialism, and self-satisfaction was brought to an end by the language of God. People, in common devotion to Jesus Christ, understood each other and were able to make themselves understood by still others.

All this is told, not simply to record an event in history, but for our benefit today. We live in a world where the forces that divide us threaten to destroy us, as they destroyed the unity of the race at Babel. The only hope for a world divided, not only by language of the tongue, but by language of the heart, is to discover a force stronger than the forces that divide us.

F. Clark Williams tells of an experience he had when he was a choir director at a small, predominantly African-American, Presbyterian college in Alabama. "I used to take the college choir on tours," he writes, "and one year we visited the Presbyterian churches in Mexico. We had sung a concert one evening at one of the churches in Monterrey, and afterward the Mexican young people took us on a tour. We were standing at the top of the Bishop's Palace overlooking Monterrey, and we couldn't really communicate. Here we were, these mostly black college students from the deep South who couldn't speak Spanish, and these Mexican Presbyterian young people who couldn't speak English, and about the only thing we had in common was that most of us were Presbyterian. We were just standing around, shuffling and fidgeting.

"Then someone started singing. Popular songs at first, and I was impressed that the popular songs of the day were known in both countries, but they ran out of those. Then someone started singing hymns. Some of the great hymns of the church like 'The Church's One Foundation,' 'Holy, Holy, Holy,' 'Amazing Grace' and we sang a lot of hymns together. Even though it was coming out in English and Spanish at the same time, we all knew what it meant. We wound up singing the 'Hallelujah Chorus' together (which they all knew). It was a beautiful night, and it was a living episode of the fact that God's love transcends all languages and all barriers of communication." In their individual awareness that each of them was a child of God, they became aware that all of them had one Father and that all of them were part of one family.

Babel stands for all that separates us from God and from one another. Pentecost expresses the unity that is possible when God's Spirit takes possession of our lives and enables us to live as family.

MOTHER'S DAY

Soul Shaping
Ephesians 6:1-4; 2 Corinthians 4:6-10

Humphrey Lee tells of an experience he had while visiting a small airport and watching a plane take off at night: "As the plane heads its nose down the runway, an airport attendant turns a switch, and a pencil of light is thrown along the path of the plane. The plane makes its way along that thread of light until it rises gracefully from the ground and makes its way into the darkness. The attendant then switches off this beam of light. He has done all that he can do (to get the plane airborne). He has not dispelled the darkness — but he has helped the pilot off to a good start." As I read that I was impressed with how analogous that experience is to parenthood. As parents we try to illuminate the path, we do what we can to help, but eventually the child is at the controls of his or her own destiny.
Virginia Satir, in her book *Peoplemaking*, expresses great compassion for parents: "Parents teach in the toughest school in the world — The School for Making People. You are the board of education, the principal, the classroom teacher, and the janitor... You are expected to be experts on all subjects pertaining to life and living. There are few schools to train you for your job, and there is no general agreement on the curriculum. You have to make it up yourself. Your school has no holidays, no vacations, no unions, no automatic promotions, or pay raises. You are on duty or at least on call 24 hours a day, 365 days a year, for at least eighteen years for each child you have." What a responsibility!

On this Mother's Day I would like all of us — mothers, fathers, extended family members — to consider how we can make the most of our soul-shaping opportunities. Not only do parents have responsibility for the physical development of their children, they are the first shapers of their children's spiritual life as well. Sometimes we do a good job of shaping our children's souls, and sometimes we do a poor job, but the family is the place where children receive their earliest and deepest convictions about the nature of God and the world. Considering the fractured nature of so many families today, we might long for a time when things were different, but today's families are the ones we have to work with. An elderly doctor listened to the complaints of a woman who was bemoaning the disappearance of the family physician, the "good old-fashioned doctor." Finally he lost patience and replied, "Madam, if you will show me an old-fashioned family, I will produce a doctor for it." The family has changed and everything that surrounds it, but the family is still the primary influence in shaping the spiritual life of the child. On this Mother's Day I would like us to consider together how we can make the most of our opportunities.

One thing a healthy home does is to enable us to experience acceptance. Unfortunately, not every home offers that experience. One teenager complained to a friend: "My dad wants me to have all the things he never had when he was a boy — including straight *A*s on my report card." When such pressures are put on children, the message they get is that they are accepted only when they succeed.

A film came out titled *Muriel's Wedding*. It depicts a dysfunctional family in which the father, who sees himself as something of a success, regularly puts his children down for their lack of accomplishment. With the family gathered in a restaurant for what we hope will be a happy meal, he publicly derides each one for stupidity, laziness, and lack of ambition. Each of us in the audience feels our own stomach turn as we agonize with the humiliated children. One soothes her damaged psyche through eating, another by vegetating in front of the television set, and a third one lives increasingly in a fantasy world planning for a glorious wedding that is unlikely to occur. The lives of each of them are twisted because no one offers to accept them as they are.

What each of us needs is to have our uniqueness affirmed. One writer shares the experience of a young man named Dennis. Dennis is a genius at fixing bicycles. He has always been a mechanical whiz. But educationally, Dennis bombed out. He simply wasn't interested. Nobody would have guessed that either, because his dad is a college professor and his mother is dean of women in the same school. While Dennis was still in high school, his mother and father said, "Son, we'd really like you to graduate. But we're going to get off your back about grades and a good record and going to college. We're proud of the way you can do things we can't do. In fact, we think you're just great. So, more than anything, we want you to be you." I don't know if that is a fairy tale or not. But most of us wish that would be the way that all families would handle such matters. When we experience unconditional acceptance, it makes the world a hopeful place. When we experience that acceptance from those whose acceptance is most important to us, it helps us to believe that God can accept us too, even when we are not perfect.

Another thing a healthy home provides is an awareness that successful living involves discipline. Discipline has to be administered in the right balance. If it's too heavy-handed, it is a turn-off. Martin Luther once said, "Whenever I say the Lord's Prayer, I always have trouble with the word 'Father' because I think of my own father, who was stern and unrelenting." Too much harsh discipline.

On the other hand, the absence of discipline is also a negative. For at least the first twenty years following World War II, Dr. Benjamin Spock was considered as the world's foremost authority on rearing children. According to his writings, parents make a grave mistake when they use any form of punishment or when they attempt to suppress the natural drives and impulses of their children. In recent years, however, Dr. Spock apologized for misleading millions of parents. He went on to say, "Inability to be firm is the most common problem of parents. I blame at least part of the resulting brattiness of children on the experts — the child psychiatrists, teachers, social workers, and pediatricians like myself. We did not realize, until it was too late, how our know-it-all attitude was undermining (the self-assurance of parents) and turning kids into brats." A Detroit judge has observed that the common denominator in the juvenile delinquents that appear before him is that they lack a strong father.

What is needed is balance. In an article in *Good Housekeeping* magazine, Dr. Joyce Brothers noted that: "Strictness has been considered an old-fashioned method of parenting, but it may be coming back into style. A recent study of almost 2,000 fifth and sixth graders — some of whom had been reared by strict parents, others by permissive ones — produced some surprising results. The children who had been strictly disciplined possessed high self-esteem and were high achievers, socially and academically. What these children said revealed that they were actually happier than the undisciplined children. They loved the adults who made and enforced the rules they lived by."

That doesn't mean the kids will make it easy for us to enforce the rules. A colleague, Calvin Miller, tells about a rule he had that his daughter, Melanie, couldn't date until she was sixteen. When she was fifteen and three fourths, the Christmas dance came along, and a boy asked her to go. When he remained firm, she became incensed and said, "Dad, I just hope that the Lord comes back between now and February so you have to live with yourself through all eternity knowing that I never had a date!"

When I was raising children, I was always interested in how to motivate kids to do what they were supposed to do. When we would come home from vacation, getting our kids to help unpack the car, unpack their suitcases, and put everything away was like pulling teeth. I finally learned to say that nobody uses the telephone until everything is put away. It worked for us. I'll pass on an even more powerful incentive. A camper tells of seeing a loaded station wagon pull into the only remaining campsite. Four youngsters leaped from the vehicle and began feverishly unloading gear and setting up a tent. The boys then rushed off to gather firewood, while the girls and their mother set up the camp stove and cooking utensils. The nearby camper marveled to the youngsters' father: "That, sir, is some display of team work." The father replied, "I have a system. No one goes to the bathroom until the camp is set up." However we accomplish it, balanced discipline in the home helps the child to learn that each of us has responsibilities and each of us is expected to contribute to the common good.

Of course, when the home is healthy, it teaches us to give and receive love. Here, too, there has to be a balance in how we show that love. It is possible to be too solicitous. Edward Handman in a *New York Times* article asks, "Is there a father anywhere who hasn't walked into a room where a child was comfortably reading and said, 'It's too warm in here'? And is there a mother alive who has not advised her adolescent or adult children, 'Don't forget to eat'? Maybe if mothers were not on hand to constantly remind their children to eat, the species would be extinct by now. Maybe that's what really happened to the dinosaurs. A psychiatrist I know," Handman continues, "a successful practitioner in his fifties, took his mother to the Metropolitan Opera in New York. After the curtain came down and they were making their way out of the lobby to his Mercedes, she turned to him and said, 'Be sure you go to the bathroom before we go to the car.'" That is too much loving concern.

On the other hand, it is possible to provide the physical necessities a child may need, but with too little love. Johnny, age four, appeared one day at the door of his father's study with a forlorn-looking chick that had apparently strayed from a neighbor's brooder. The father said rather sternly, "John, take that chicken right back to its mother." "It ain't got no mother," Johnny replied. The father, insisting that he be obeyed, said, "Well, take it back to its father then." But Johnny protested, "It hasn't got no father either. It hasn't got anything but an old lamp!" An electric lamp may serve the physical needs of the chick well enough. It may hatch the egg and preserve the chick until it is old enough to face life. But that is about all. The tragedy is that there are some parents like that. They give their children a warm bed, nourishing meals, adequate clothing and shelter — but that is all: no love, no affection, no security! When we don't receive healthy love, it's difficult to know how to show it.

The family is the context in which most of us will make our impact upon the world. When Mother Teresa received her Nobel Prize, someone asked her, "What can we do to help promote world peace?" her answer was "Go home and love your family." The writer of the First Letter of John reminds us that if we do not love our brother, whom we have seen, we cannot love God whom we have not seen (1 John 4:20). We learn how to love in the family, and it prepares us to love God.

Indeed, it is the actions, symbols, and rituals we experience in the family that bring us to an awareness of God. There is no getting away from the fact that what the parents value has an impact on their children. Larry Christenson, writing about the Christian family, states that "the family belongs to God. God created it. God determined its inner structure.... By divine permission, a man and a woman may cooperate with God's purpose and become a part of it. But the home they establish remains God's establishment. Thus it is not our marriage, but God's marriage; not our home, but God's home; not our children, but God's children; not our family, but God's family." This might sound like pious rhetoric, but it works itself out in thoroughly down-to-earth fashion. If Jesus is truly Lord in your family, it will influence everything from the way you decorate your house to the way you spend your summer vacation.

For example, the way parents respond to nature gives children a sense of reverence for nature and its creator. I read of one family that has a special table where children can place things they find to be interesting — a leaf, a feather, a shell, an unusual rock. It becomes their altar of thanks to the creator for the beauty that we find in our world.

The kinds of rituals in which we participate communicate more than words. The making and lighting of an Advent wreath or the movement of figures in a nativity scene as we move through Advent are visual reminders of the faith story.

Parental participation in worship prepares the child to see this as an important source of spiritual growth. A recent study disclosed that if both Mom and Dad attended church regularly, 72% of their children remain faithful to the church. It also showed that if only Dad attends regularly, 55% remain faithful. If only Mom attends regularly, 15% remain faithful. If neither attend regularly, only 6% remain faithful. If parents demonstrate their stewardship by showing their children how they give regularly of their resources and encourage the children to give of their own substance, it promotes sharing and overcomes the normal human tendency to want to keep what we have for ourselves. Children need to see their parents buying and contributing food to the church food closet, contributing to the Salvation Army bell ringer's bucket, donating blood because someone needs it.

Whatever we do, good or bad, we make an impression on our children. Dr. William Farson (quoted in *Redbook* magazine, September 1977) speaking about parental influence, says that we are tempted to think that we can shape our children the way a sculptor shapes clay. But that is not the way it is. He says it is more like we are running along and we fall on a pile of clay. "We leave an impression all right," he says, "and that impression is distinctly us, but we have very little control over what it looks like. You see, in child raising what parents *are* is terribly important. I suspect that kindness and decency, for instance, are learned by being around mothers and fathers who are kind and decent, and the same is true of other qualities."

It is an awesome responsibility. We leave an impression on our children through what we are. They will be uniquely who they are, but what they are will be influenced by what we are. May God help us to be all we can be.

BIBLE SUNDAY

Does God Have a Word for You!
2 Timothy 3:14-17

When our children were growing up we tried to sit down to breakfast at the same time so that we might begin the day on the same track. However, as the girls got older it became increasingly difficult for us to accomplish. Even though each one knew that breakfast would be served, we didn't all make it to the table at the same time. My wife would call from the kitchen, "Breakfast is ready." But someone would be in the shower and wouldn't hear. Someone would be using a blow dryer and not respond. Another might be looking for something out in the garage and would be too far away to hear. The message was given, but it wasn't heard.

When the obstacles to communication were overcome, and people did manage to get to the table, it was not the *message* about the food which nourished us, it was the food itself. And the food would not automatically give nourishment: It had to be lifted to the mouth; it involved some personal effort. Then, too, as individuals we would have our own preferences. A person might take more of one thing, less of another, none of something else, even though what was not taken might be good for them. This situation could be further expanded, but the intention of this message is not to describe the problems connected with getting breakfast.

What I want to suggest is that God has a word for each of us, but as with the message to come to the table, the message from God is often missed: a) we may not hear it; b) we may misinterpret what it says; c) we may mistake the form of the message for its content; d) we may hear the message, but fail to avail ourselves of it, so that it proves worthless to us.

Historically, the church has maintained that God speaks to us through the Bible. God may speak to us in other ways too, but since the Reformation, at least, Protestant Christians have felt that the Bible has a central place in God's efforts to communicate with people. Many of us may feel that we have not heard the message. I would like to suggest that there are some things we can do to get the message the Bible has for us.

For one thing, we need to approach the Bible receptively. That means that we must expect to get something. If we don't expect to get fed, we probably won't even come to the table. The psalmist prayed: "Open my eyes that I may behold wonderful things out of thy law" (Psalm 119:18). A missionary in Mexico, Gonzolo Baez-Camargo, tells of a group of Indians he discovered in a remote village. Years before he came to the village, some of the Indians had been doing some trading on the outskirts of Tampico. While there, they saw a colporteur, a seller of Bibles, being attacked by some fanatics who didn't want him selling Bibles in Mexico. The Bibles were torn apart. The Indians, watching the fight, realized that the fight had started over the books. They picked up some of the pieces and took them back to the leader of their village, who recognized them as having come from the Bible. "When I was in the hospital I was visited by a woman who gave me one of these books," he said. The Indians thought that if that book was worth fighting for, it must be worth something. They eventually got hold of a copy and shared its contents with the rest of the villagers. When the missionary came to that village years later he discovered that practically all the inhabitants were Christians. They read the Bible receptively, and they found food for their souls and for the souls of others.

To approach the Bible receptively, however, does not mean that we have to approach it uncritically. The Reformers sought to establish the authority of the Bible over all other sources of Christian faith and doctrine. In order to enhance that authority, the church emphasized the divine origin of the book by playing down the human instruments who wrote it. Instead of saying of the Bible that it *contained* the word of God, it became more and more assumed that the Bible *was* the word of God, right down to the last letter. To say that the Bible was inspired came to mean that it was dictated, and therefore infallible. The Reformers had wanted to get away from the tyranny of an infallible pope, but many of the Protestants who followed in their train, anxious for some absolute authority, have insisted on an infallible book, which has become to them a paper pope to be obeyed uncritically.

Yet, Martin Luther, who certainly upheld the authority of the Bible, likened the Bible to the manger that held Christ: people bowed before the manger, not because *it* was worthy of devotion, but because of the *Christ* who was in it. "In a similar way," he said, "the Bible contains the word of God — supremely revealed to us in Jesus Christ — but the Bible is not at all points the same as the word of God, and in some of its content it may have no more value for us than the manger that held Christ."

I submit that it is possible to say that the Bible is inspired, and yet be discriminating about its contents. It is possible to read it as a record of the spiritual experiences of people who, over the twelve centuries spanned by its writing, were guided, supported, chastened, forgiven, redeemed, and delivered by God. It is possible to acknowledge that it contains God's self-revelation, God's disclosure of himself and his will, and yet to acknowledge that its message comes to us through channels of human fallibility mixed with great insight. It has a heavenly message, but it is contained in an earthen vessel. We must approach it receptively, but also with discrimination.

A second way to get the word for ourselves is to study the Bible within the fellowship of the church. This doesn't rule out Bible study on our own. It is simply following the admonition of Peter that "no prophecy of scripture is a matter of one's own interpretation" (2 Peter 1:20).

Any kind of study is benefited by consideration of what others have found. It would be foolish to study medicine as though no one had ever studied it before. In any branch of science the first thing we do is acquaint ourselves with what has been discovered heretofore. In studying the Bible it would be folly to neglect the scholarship and devotion of the past. We also need the response of other people to what we think we have discovered. We need to hear God's Spirit speak through the opinions of others. Luther held that Jerome's Latin Bible, the Bible of the Church for some 1,000 years, was not a good translation because Jerome had produced it alone and thereby lost the promise that where two or three are gathered in his name, Jesus Christ is with them. The study of the Bible in the company of others is richer than the study of the Bible in isolation. To that end, in this church we offer numerous opportunities through the year to study the Bible with others.

Another thing we must be prepared to do is to approach the Bible with an open mind. That means we study to seek truth, not to prove a case about which we have already made up our minds. Unfortunately, a person can use the Bible to find in it what he or she wants to find. One can use it to hear the echo of one's own voice rather than the voice of God. Jacob Arminuis, the theologian upon whose work much of the Methodist point of view is built, once said: "Nothing is more obstructive to the investigation of the truth than prior commitments to partial truths."

With an open mind we are not afraid to ask questions such as: "Who wrote these words? Who first read them? What situation were they facing? What was the meaning to the writer? Is this statement still applicable to us?"

A grown woman had for years been cutting the end off of a ham before baking it because she had seen her mother do it. When she was teaching her own daughter to cook, the girl asked why she did that. She said she didn't know, but she would find out. She called her mother and asked, "Mother why do you always cut the end off of the ham before baking it?" "Simple," said the mother. "I only had a short pan."

People observed that John Calvin, the Scottish Reformer, always covered his head when he went into a church. "It is to show his piety," said his students, and they followed suit. One day an uninitiated student asked him, "Why do you cover your head when you go into church?" "Simple," said Calvin. "Because of the pigeons." In a similar way, some things are to be found in the Bible that were appropriate when written, but which are not so appropriate now. If we approach the Bible with an open mind, some of our cherished ideas, practices, and opinions may have to be challenged so that new truths can appear.

A further thing we must do in order to understand God's word for ourselves is to acknowledge that the human understanding of God's revelation has been a developing thing. This has traditionally been called "progressive revelation." It means that, in the history of the race, God has had to deal with human beings at the level of their development or ability to receive truth. As simple arithmetic precedes calculus, so sub-Christian attitudes preceded Christian ones. For example, it is possible to find in earlier sections of the Bible that the execution of prisoners of war and the mutilation of slaves and criminals is condoned. These are actions or ideas that represent the stage at which people had arrived at that time. We do not need to defend those things as being part of the unchanging will of God. More than once Jesus said: "You have heard it said thus and so, but I say to you..." (Matthew 5:21ff) and he challenges the old teaching with a new one.

Christians generally believe that with the coming of Jesus Christ some things have been left behind. The early Jews, for example, tried to answer the question, "How do we show our religion?" They did this by abstaining from certain kinds of food such as pork; they wore tasseled garments, or bound copies of the law to their wrists; they circumcised their male children. These were honorable attempts to show their faith, but Christians believe that the fuller revelation came in Jesus, who taught "by this shall all people know that you are my disciples, if you have love for one another" (John 13:35). Love is the fuller revelation.

What this means for Christians is that our understanding of God has developed over the centuries. For us, the New Testament interprets the Old Testament. For us, some ideas have been sloughed off and not followed up, because they did not move in a profitable direction. For us, the idea is not so much the letter of the text as the spirit revealed in Jesus Christ. Therefore, the fact that a statement is found in the Bible does not necessarily make it true for today. What makes a statement true is that it comes from God. Our best knowledge of whether it comes from God is if it accords with the words, the mind, and the life of Christ.

Again, we need to acknowledge that we are dealing with varying types of literature in the Bible. Indeed, the Bible is not a book but a library. It is composed of 66 books, written by many authors, over a period of more than a thousand years, and in several languages. Some portions are intended as history, though often biased; some portions are intended as poetry, and not to be taken literally; some portions are fables, allegories, short stories, oratory, letters, and so forth.

To interpret them all alike is to do injustice to the message. For example, in the book of Joshua it is written that "Joshua spoke to God saying: 'Sun, stand still at Gibeon; And Moon in the valley of Ajalon.' And the sun stood still, and the moon stayed, until the nation took vengeance on their enemies" (Joshua 10:12).

What we have here is a poetic quotation, and the poet is using the same kind of license we use when we say, "that was the longest hour of my life," even though it was no longer or shorter than any other hour. In our desire to take the Bible seriously, we do not have to believe that there was a day when the sun stood still. We do the Bible a disservice when we treat the beauty of its poetry as though it were a description of historical fact.

We also need to be aware that the point of view of the writers helped to shape what they wrote. They had a worldview different from our own. As far as they were concerned, the earth was the center of things. The sky was a dome over the earth, and the netherworld was beneath. But the truth of what they have to say is not bound by their worldview. The important thing is what they believed humanity to be like; what they believed God to be like; and that whatever the earth is like, the creating power of God is behind it all.

When we finally overcome the various obstacles to our understanding and begin to read the Bible, there is still one more thing we have to do: We have to learn to put what we read into action. During World War II, an American flyer was forced to parachute into the ocean near an island in the South Seas. Several days later he saw one of the islanders reading the Bible. "Gosh, do you have that book out here?" he asked. "If we didn't," said the islander, "you would have been eaten by now." Here were people who not only read the Bible, they responded to it by their actions.

In the Bible God speaks to us through people and events, not to give us a history lesson, but to give us a message and to solicit a response. The message is: "I love you." God is waiting for our response.

MEMORIAL SUNDAY

Heroes
Hebrews 11:1—12:2

In the Olympic Games a few years ago, a runner on one of the relay teams dropped the baton and thereby dashed the hopes of his teammates. He lay down on the track and wept. So much had gone into their preparation that the sense of responsibility and loss was enormous.

The author of the book of Hebrews must have had in mind a similar situation when he set out to describe the way the faith has come down to us, from one quaking hand to the next. He conceives of many of the characters of the Old Testament as participants in this race which has relayed the faith to us. In the course of constructing his argument, he says some interesting things about faith and about our responsibility for passing it on. Many of the people he uses for examples of faith have become known as heroes of the faith, even though many of them were not very heroic. It occurs to me that Memorial Sunday is a good time to consider some of the heroes of our faith so that we might be guided by whatever their lives have to say to us.

The first thing the author has us do is to look at the team. It is apparent that there are some weaknesses among the team members. For example, some lack the purity that we might expect of examples of faith. He speaks of Rahab the prostitute. She was the woman who lived in Jericho when some Israelite spies came to spy out the defenses of the city before Joshua led the people against it on their way to settle in Palestine. She hid the spies in her brothel when they were being sought by Jericho's officers, and she lied on their behalf. Later, she attached herself to the Israelites and became the wife of one of them. But she doesn't seem like a noteworthy example of faith. The author also mentions Jephthah. He was the illegitimate son of a prostitute, an outlaw chieftain, who fought successfully against one of Israel's enemies, the Ammonites. Flushed with victory, he foolishly vowed to sacrifice the first thing that he saw when he arrived home. It turned out to be his own daughter. Not quite what you'd expect as an example of faith.

Not only were some lacking in purity, some of the heroes were not too intelligent. There was big, burly Samson — a physical wonder, but an intellectual midget. He fought against the Philistines, but he was repeatedly deceived by wily women, until he eventually lost his sight and his strength. He made one big comeback, but for the purpose of revenge, and in the process killed himself. Not too exemplary.

Then too not all of these heroes were courageous. There was a day, we are reminded, when a man couldn't be found to lead Israel against her enemies, so a woman, Deborah, took the responsibility. Through shame, she caused a man by the name of Barak to take command of Israel's forces. He did and was victorious, but as Deborah said, it would be a woman who would be responsible for the victory. Yet that man, Barak, is lifted up as an example of faith.

Of course, some of the team members did have spectacular victories. The author speaks of those who stopped the mouths of lions; no doubt a reference to Daniel, whom the lions did not eat when he was thrown into their den for refusing to worship an idol. He mentions David, Israel's most illustrious king, who started out as a shepherd boy and made good. He speaks of those made strong in weakness, perhaps a reference to Judith, a lovely young widow in Israel who made her way to the enemy camp, beguiled the enemy general, and killed him. He speaks of women who received their dead by resurrection — an incident which happened in the life of Elijah, the prophet, when he restored to life a young boy who apparently was dead. And he speaks of those who put foreign armies to flight, perhaps a reference to the Maccabees, who led the Israelites to rebel against the Syrian oppressors and brought in a period of independence. Those kinds of heroes we can understand. Whether they seem to be heroes of faith or not, at least it seems plausible that God was with them.

There is one thing that all of those whom we have mentioned

have in common: They are all a part of the past. We know what their performance was. What is still uncertain is the performance of the present and future members of the team — and that involves us.

A second thing we might look at is the track on which the race takes place. In the past there have been some really rough spots as participants have run their course. Some people have been mocked. Among them our author mentions Noah — that fellow who built a boat on dry ground in preparation for the big rain. His neighbors mocked and taunted him all the while he was building. Some people have been imprisoned — like Jeremiah. He was thrown into an unused well and kept there, up to his armpits in mud for days, because he told the truth as he saw it. Some were forced to wander in the desert, living in caves and wearing animal skins. These were wandering bands of prophets who were persecuted for their faith and had to flee from place to place. Some were stoned to death, the author says. Zechariah, the priest, was caught by an angry mob in the temple courtyard and stoned for calling the people to give an accounting for their faithlessness. And Steven, the first martyr of the Christian church, was stoned for declaring his faith in Jesus Christ. Some were even sawed in two. There is a tradition that the prophet Isaiah was placed inside a hollow tree by order of cruel King Manasseh, who then had the tree cut in two, because the prophet would not approve of the king's idolatry or take part in it. It is not difficult, then, to acknowledge that there have been many rough spots along the course on which our faith has been transmitted.

It is apparent that not everyone responded to the course in the same way. Abel, the son of Adam, presented a sacrifice in devotion to God and it was accepted. Abraham moved from Mesopotamia to Palestine in search of a place to raise his family. Moses, raised as an Egyptian prince by Pharaoh's daughter, renounced his opportunities and chose instead to share the ill treatment of the people of Israel. All of these people were responding in faith — but they responded differently as their circumstances dictated. Our circumstances, in turn, are vastly different from theirs so that were we to respond in faith, it would not mean that we would do any of the things that they did. But there is a common thread running through their actions which it would be helpful for us to note. The common thread is that each person ran the race in his or her own style, but everyone passed on the baton.

Therefore, let us look next at the baton that is passed between the runners, a baton called faith. That faith involved action. In some quarters it seems to be taught that faith simply means subscribing to certain beliefs, regardless of conduct. I read about a certain man who loved to go to revivals. He loved to get up and testify. He made his witness over and over again, publicly admitting his past sinful life. He had done it all — lied, cheated, stolen, pushed dope, spent time in jail, broken all the Ten Commandments and then some! It was his custom at the end of his long recital of wrongdoing to smile and say, "I thank God through all those wicked years I never lost my religion." Obviously, for that man, faith was simply a matter of believing something, regardless of whether it affected his conduct. All of those heroes we have talked about didn't share a common statement of faith, but what they believed influenced their actions.

The faith that they passed on was an attitude of trust in what God had already done in the past making it possible to trust that God would also act in the future. Abraham was promised a land and a populous nation, but the only land he owned at his death was a burial plot he had to buy, and his nation was one son. Moses was to lead his people to a land of their own, but he did not get to enter it. He was only able to see it in the distance. United Methodist Bishop Woodie White tells of one of the most difficult things he has ever faced. He was sitting home in his easy chair, watching a football game, when the phone rang. "Woodie! Woodie!" his sister screamed hysterically. "You better come quick! Something has happened to mother!" White left at once on the long drive to his mother's house. "What possibly could have happened? Had she fallen? Why was his sister so hysterical?" He was concerned and tried to prepare himself — but nothing could have prepared him for what he found. His 73-year-old mother had been violently attacked. Someone had broken into her home and brutally beaten her, robbed her, and physically abused her. Her face was bruised and bloody. Her clothes were torn. Her eyes were swollen almost shut. Bishop White could not believe what he was seeing; at first he stood there in a state of shock. Then he ran to her, threw his arms around her, and began to cry. And then something strange and special happened. As he was holding his mother, he detected a familiar aroma. "Mother," he said, "What is that I'm smelling?" and she answered, "It's fried chicken, son. I thought you might be hungry after your long drive." Woodie White could hardly believe that his mother would think about him in the face of this horrible tragedy. He broke into tears again and hugged his mother tightly. She looked up at him, her face aglow. "Son," she said, "I want to tell you something, and I don't want you to ever forget it. God is still good! God is still good! God is still good!" There was one who saw eye-to-eye with the writer of Hebrews: "Faith is the substance of things hoped for, the evidence of things not seen." She was passing on the baton.

The final thing we might look at this morning is team spirit, and that is where we come in. If we want to be listed among the people of faith, we have a responsibility to the past. Apart from us, the efforts of those who have gone before us cannot come to completion. Isaac, in his age and blindness, blessed Jacob and foretold a time of greatness. Jacob, on his deathbed in Egypt, assembled his twelve sons and uttered blessings involving things yet to be. Gideon, Barak, Samson, Jephthah experienced victories, but the ultimate victory of good over evil was still future. David expanded a kingdom, but the coming kingdom of God was still future. Some may have stopped the mouths of lions for a while, but there was still death to be faced at a later date.

Of all of them it may be said that they never lost their vision or their hope. "All these died in faith," says the author, "not having received what was promised, but having seen it and greeted it from afar, acknowledging that they were strangers and exiles on the earth." Our author gives the impression that as previous runners have passed on the baton of faith, that is, hopefulness, trust in God, they have left the field and entered the stands where they now cheer us on. Therefore, we are not involved in a lonely struggle. We are surrounded by those witnesses who have gone before. By the record of their lives they reassure us that endurance is possible, hardship at its worst is limited, and the grace of God can sustain us. And in that great cloud of witnesses may also be found our mothers and fathers, our husbands and wives, our sisters and brothers, our sons and daughters, cheering us on so that we do not drop the baton or give up too soon, for what they have invested is advanced by what we do.

If we want to be listed among the people of faith, we also have a responsibility to those who come after us. We must pass on something to those who come after. If we drop the baton, it affects others. After describing Abel's acceptable sacrifice, the author says Abel died, but through his faith he is speaking yet. In 1858 a Sunday school teacher named Mr. Kimball led a shoe clerk to give his life to Christ. The clerk was Dwight L. Moody. Moody became an evangelist in England and in 1879 awakened the heart of Fredrick Meyer, then pastor of a small church. Pastor Meyer came to America and while preaching on a college campus won J. Wilbur Chapman to Christ. Wilbur Chapman became a YMCA worker and picked up a former baseball player to do evangelistic work. That player was named Billy Sunday. At a revival in Charlotte, North Carolina, Sunday so excited a group of local men that they engaged Mordecai Hamm to come to their town. In the revival with Mordecai Hamm, a young man heard the gospel and yielded his life to Christ. His name was Billy Graham.

Every one of us, when we come to our particular finish line, will pass on something for good or ill. God grant that what we leave behind becomes a blessing to those who come after us.

So in us the race comes to the present moment. Others are looking to us to carry forward toward fulfillment the vision they had. And we discover that, given seventy or even a hundred years, we shall not fully arrive either, but hopefully, we shall have advanced the vision of what is yet to be by putting our trust in God's ability to bring it to pass. Then to those who are to come after us, we say in words of John McCrae, "To you, from failing hands, we throw the torch; be yours to hold it high."

MUSIC / CHOIR RECOGNITION SUNDAY

Say It With Music
Ephesians 5:17-20

When I was in college I had a roommate who could sing from memory most of the great arias from grand opera in Italian, though he did not speak Italian. I asked him how he could do that. He said that from the time he was an infant, his parents had played opera on the phonograph day after day. "Anyone who is exposed to classical music while a child will grow up loving it," he said.

I filed the idea away, and when our first child was born, my wife and I decided we would expose our children daily to classical music. I have to tell you that the jury is still out on the results of that noble experiment. When they became old enough to buy their own tapes, the only thing they were interested in was rock music. While they were growing up, whenever I got the chance to drive the family car after they had been using it, I would turn on the ignition and the radio or tape deck that had been left on would explode with sound that had about as much relationship to music as the take off of a jet airplane. When I would talk with them about what they were listening to, they would say, "Really, Dad, rock music is better than it sounds." Over the years, as I have tried small, digestible doses of their music, I have occasionally discovered something to which I could relate. Interestingly enough, I notice that on occasion one of my daughters buys something by Rachmaninoff or Mozart. I'm just waiting for the day when one of them says to me, "You know, Dad, classical music isn't as bad as it sounds."

Each of us probably has some kind of music that we enjoy hating. For some, it may be country and western; for others it may be opera. Though we may not like this or that kind of music, it is hard to imagine anyone being opposed to all kinds of music. Yet, there are some people who are opposed to music in general. One such person was the Ayatollah Khomeini. He declared that "music is no different from opium," and he banned music from Iranian broadcasting. Khomeini said, "If you want your country to be independent you must turn radio and television into educational institutions and eliminate music. Music makes the brain inactive."

Plato is probably the founding father of the anti-music department. Like the Ayatollah, Plato thought that music lulled the best part of the soul into relaxing its guard. Music, he maintained, gratified the emotions and thus weakens and distracts the good citizens.

Standing between Plato and Khomeini is Saint Augustine, another anti-music person. He equated the "delights of the ears" with the "contentment of the flesh," and knowing his own susceptibility to such things, he recommended that "the whole melody of sweet music" be banished from his ears and from the church's too.

Fortunately for posterity there have been those in the church who have disagreed with Saint Augustine. In Paul's letter to the Ephesians, he urged the Ephesian Christians to "... be filled with the Spirit, addressing one another in psalms, hymns, and spiritual songs, singing and making melody to the Lord with all your heart." Music in Paul's day and ever since, has been a vital element of worship and an important part of the daily expression of faith for the people of God. It has always been in song that people have most clearly expressed their feelings and their faith. In Psalm 98 the psalmist urges us to sing songs of praise. It is the place of music in the praise of God that I should like to have us consider together today.

The first thing that I want to point out is that it is good for us to sing songs of praise because songs speak to us. Music affects our outlook. Hans Christian Anderson, in his tale *The Nightengale* expresses the power which music exercises over the human heart. He has the Nightengale say to the saddened emperor of Japan, "I will sing to you and make you thoughtful. I will sing to you of the happy ones and of those who suffer. I will sing about the good and the evil..." Music gets us ready to respond to any subject, and those who want a certain response know how to use music to get us in the mood. Trumpets speak of kings, drums speak of armies, and soft violins create the setting for tender emotions.

Leonard Bernstein once noted that the value of a musical work doesn't lie in its physical structure but in the affect that it has on us. Describing the evolution of New Orleans jazz, Alan Lomax, a musicologist, notes: "The late 1900s were hard times for blacks in the south. There had been a lot of killing. What little was left of their strength was concentrated in early New Orleans black lodges. They organized marching bands to play at funerals... and in putting together these lodge bands the New Orleans blacks went back to their ancestral roots. Their bands were full of horns and drums... They spoke through them. It was a language, and also an assertion of male strength and power. Black males were marching again as if they were back in Africa. They hadn't been able to do that during the whole of slavery." Music was setting the stage for a time when a previously dispirited group of people would rise up and affirm, "Black is beautiful."

Music prepares all of us to receive the good news. Martin Luther possessed a great love of music, was well-trained in it, and showed a remarkable understanding of its nature. "I truly desire," he said, "that all Christians would love and regard as worthy the lovely gift of music... (for) next to the word of God, the noble art of music is the greatest treasure in this world. It controls our thoughts, minds, hearts, and spirits." Like the early church leaders, Luther saw music as a means of making the believer more receptive to the Christian faith, for, as he put it, "God has his gospel preached... through the gift of music." For him, music was a servant of the church whose function was to give greater significance to the text. Songs of praise speak to us.

The second thing that I want to say is that songs of praise help us to express what is in us. For example, they express feelings of faith. When I visit some of the old cathedrals of Europe, I am surprised to see how the choir stalls are situated in such a way that what the choir was doing was not visible to most of the worshipers in the church. The choir sang its songs of praise to God while most of the people in the church just wandered around with no particular involvement. The medieval church apparently saw the faithful as spectators before the holy mysteries, simply passive listeners, and the church was weak because of it. With the coming of the Reformation, the church's songs of proclamation, praise, and thanksgiving were returned to the people. From that point on, Protestant worship was to involve the people, for only by involvement and personal expression could people feel that they had worshiped rather than been entertained.

There are things in us that words alone cannot express. A man once wrote to Albert Einstein and asked him to describe the theory of relativity in simple words so that the man might at least catch a glimpse of its meaning. Einstein answered him back by saying that he could not do what the man requested, but if the man would call on him at his home in Princeton, Einstein would play it on his violin.

Human words do have their limitations, limitations which are overcome by music. In 1977 two remarkable spacecrafts named *Voyager* were launched with the purpose of exploring Jupiter and Saturn and then to leave the solar system and cruise for eons through the realms of other stars. Affixed to each is a gold-coated phonograph record containing 87-1/2 minutes of music from our planet. The music included ranges from Bach and Beethoven to a pygmy initiation rite. Carl Sagan, who was responsible for collecting the music to be included, noted with delight: "Our previous messages had contained information about how we perceive ourselves and how we think. But we are feeling creatures. Music, it seemed to me, was at least a creditable attempt to convey human emotions." And so, somewhere in space, a spacecraft reaches out to other beings and says, "We were here, and music expresses what we felt." Perhaps this truth is what Paul recognized when he urged his fellow Christians to use music in expressing their faith. Songs of praise give us a chance to express what is in us.

The third thing I want to say is that it is good to sing songs of praise because they keep us focused on God. Music seems to be a basic ingredient of the universe. The psalmist, with an ear turned heavenward, wrote:

The heavens are telling the glory of God; and the firmament proclaims his handiwork. Day to day pours forth speech, and night to night declares knowledge. There is no speech, nor are there words; their voice is not heard; yet their voice goes out through all the earth, and their words to the end of the world.
(Psalm 19:1-4)

In an unscientific age he was aware of the music of the spheres.

In an essay titled *A New Song*, Harold Dekker has suggested that the universe is literally full of music. As the psalmist wrote so poetically, space is saturated with sound. Melody is everywhere and rhythmic tones are in the air all the time. But most of this music cannot be heard with the human ear. Sound is produced by vibrations in the air, measured by their number per second. Our human ears catch sounds ranging between 16,000 and 30,000 vibrations per second. Below that range are countless sounds that we miss, and above it there are sounds so vast that their unheard chorus is beyond imagination. Perhaps you were struck as I was by the use of music in the film, *Close Encounters of the Third Kind*, not only as an international language but as a vehicle of communication among unlike creatures inhabiting outer space. The suggestion was that there is a basic harmony in the universe that draws us together. It seems so very appropriate that we earthlings should use the vehicle of music to express our praise of the God of the whole universe.

I close with this. I read recently that when Jenny Lind, who was known as the Swedish nightingale, was coming to this country for her first concert tour, she expressed to the captain of the ship bringing her from Europe a desire to see a sunrise at sea. In accordance with her wish, one cloudless morning he had her called at first dawn. Silent and motionless she stood on the deck watching every change of shade and tint in the sky until the first golden rays shot up from the horizon. As the sun leaped up from the waves, Jenny Lind burst into rapturous song, her deeply religious feeling finding expression in the noble music of Handel's *Messiah*. She seemed oblivious to the gathering onlookers. In the ecstasy of her emotion she lifted her voice to an unseen hearer, to whose majesty and glory she paid her tribute. In telling of the experience later, the captain described the scene and exclaimed later, "No one will ever hear 'I Know That My Redeemer Liveth,'" sung as we heard it that morning.

There is a unique capacity in music to speak to us, to express what is in us, to direct our attention to the God of creation. Let us always be ready to do as the psalmist says: To raise our voices in songs of praise.

FATHER'S DAY

Good Foundations
Ephesians 5:25—6:4

A little girl in the second grade was asked by her teacher to write a paper about her personal hero. She came home with a paper she had written about her father. The father was flattered by the choice and asked her, "Why did you pick me?" "Because," she said, "I couldn't spell Arnold Schwarzenegger."

Fathers would like to be heroes to their children, or failing that, at least to feel that they have done their best to give their family a good foundation. In Paul's letter to the Ephesians, he gives several suggestions about what goes into a good foundation.

The first thing Paul says is, "Husbands, love your wives." That means we continue to nurture our spouse throughout our marriage. Religion writer Bruce Larson tells about the change in relationship between husband and wife after they have been married for a few years. He illustrates this by relating the seven stages of the common cold in the life of a young married couple. The first year, the husband says, "Sugar, I'm worried about my little sweetie pie. You've got a bad sniffle and I want to put you in the hospital for a complete checkup." The second year, the husband says: "Listen, honey, I don't like the sound of that cough. I've called the doctor and he's going to rush right over." The third year, it goes like this: "Maybe you'd better lie down, honey. Nothing like a little rest if you're feeling bad. I'll even bring you something to eat." The fourth year: "Look, dear, be sensible; after you've fed the kids and washed the dishes, you'd better hit the sack." Fifth year: "Why don't you take a couple of aspirin?" Sixth year: "If you'd just gargle or something instead of sitting around barking like a seal, it might help." Seventh year: "For heaven's sake, stop sneezing! What are you trying to do, give me pneumonia?"

It is amazing that when we are courting we can think of all the right things to say or do to win a partner, and then, when we have been married a while, forget how meaningful those words and actions were to our mate.

By nature men seem to have a harder time than women in saying the things their spouse wants to hear. There is a story, probably told by a disgruntled wife, that in the early days of creation, Eve came up to Adam in the Garden of Eden and asked, "Do you love me, Adam?" To which Adam is alleged to have responded, "Who else?" Not a very convincing display of affection, even if there were no other choices. Winston Churchill, who admittedly had a way with words, is reported to have said, when he had been married many years: "My most brilliant achievement was my ability to be able to persuade my wife to marry me," and "My marriage was much the most fortunate and joyous event which happened to me in the whole of my life." Any wife would love to hear that said about her.

Or if words do not come easily to us, let us keep romance alive by our actions. In the first edition of Edith Wharton's novel, *The Age of Innocence*, she made a glaring mistake. She quoted what she supposed to be the opening portion of the marriage service in the Prayer Book. In reality, it was the beginning of the burial service. In subsequent editions it was corrected. Nevertheless, some marriage ceremonies do seem to be burial services for any further expression of romance in the marriage. Every couple should get out of town together periodically through the year: have time away from the children, see movies, eat quiet meals together, sleep late, do what pleases them. It does wonders for their relationship and for the whole family.

Every so often my wife defines for me what she means by being romantic by relating this story. When Alan Alda and his wife, Arlene, celebrated their sixteenth wedding anniversary, they had some guests over, and one of them said he had to catch a midnight plane. Alan offered to drive him to the airport and asked Arlene to come along. At the gate Alan turned to her, pulled two plane tickets out of his pocket and said, "He isn't leaving, we are." And that was how Arlene found out Alan had secretly arranged a dream of hers: to go with him to Paris. He had taken care of her passport, rescheduled her appointments, packed her bags, and hired a sitter to stay with their daughters. I can't figure out why my wife keeps using that example.

Even if we don't fly off to Paris, romance is kept alive in other ways. It includes anything that lets our spouse know that she really counts, she isn't taken for granted, and she is really appreciated. It's a "thank you" to whoever prepared the meal; it's sharing in doing the dishes, it's putting aside the paper in order to talk; it's demonstrating to the other person, "I like to be with you." It is sharing deep experiences too. A lady of 47 who has been married 27 years and has six children said: "Love is what you've been through with somebody." Indeed it is. But romantic moments give us good memories in the tough times, and something to look forward to.

Children need to know that their father and mother are lovers. It not only gives the children stability, it demonstrates how the children's love can be expressed in their future marriage, and in so doing it contributes to the happiness of future generations.

The second thing Paul does in this passage is to remind us of the importance of communication in the home. Paul describes the marriage partners as "one flesh," indicating that they are to share themselves freely with each other, which includes interests, desires, hopes, and fears. That is called communication. I read about a man who had just installed his first Citizen Band radio in his car and was trying it out as he drove down a country road. After he had fiddled with switches and dials and shouted into his microphone for ten or fifteen minutes with no result, his wife said to him, "If you are so desperate to communicate with someone, how about if you quit fooling with that thing and talk to me?" We can get so caught up in other interests that we forget to share with the one closest to us.

Communication involves listening. Wilma Bryant in a *Reader's Digest* article tells how important it was to have someone listen to her as she grew up. "The funeral was over and it was time to sort out my father's desk, which was so forbidding to me as a child. Then I found the tattered notebook he had always carried. I read slowly, 'red bicycle,' 'roller skates,' 'birthstone ring,' 'high heels.' Whenever I just *had* to have something, I'd ask my father for it. After debating the situation, he would produce the book. All details were recorded:

color, size, cost, and my reason for really needing it. As he closed the book, Pop would look at me and say, 'Now, on my next trip to New York, I'll be sure to get it.' To many men making a living on a small farm in those Depression days, a child's world of desire would seem unimportant. Yet, those small chats set the pace for my future. In his own way, he gave me the ability to distinguish between reality and fantasy. Deep inside, I realized he would never go to New York. The important fact to me remains — Pop listened."

Communicating involves taking time. Edward Stein in his book *Fathering, Fact or Fable*, tells how that was brought home to him. "I cannot easily forget," he writes, "an illuminating personal vignette that occurred when I was in the throes of multiple early professional commitments and using most weekends to write a doctoral dissertation. My second son, then about five years of age, said one day to his six-year-old brother, 'Let's play Daddy.' I was all eyes and ears over what was to ensue. The younger one went into his bedroom, came rushing into the living room, grabbed my hat, slapped it on his head, frantically rushed around till he found my briefcase, then dashed out the front door, slamming it behind him. After that little drama, I slashed my way through my date book and wrote in 'family' here and there." We need to communicate to those who are important to us that they are important to us and that is done through actions as well as words.

In communicating we give ourselves. A colleague in ministry tells the story about his five-year-old daughter who, one day as he returned from the office, asked, "Daddy, are you going to stay home tonight?" He answered no, he had an engagement to speak at the local PTA. She was so disappointed that her father was not going to be home that evening. He thought that he would brighten her spirits by asking her to help him in writing his speech for the evening. He told her that his subject was "the ideal father," and asked her what she thought an ideal father ought to be like. She thought for a moment and said, "An ideal father is a father that knows how to fly a kite." He made notes and remembered that not too long ago they had purchased a kite and gone out to fly it together. He said, "What else?" She answered, "A good father knows how to build a fire."

Again he made notes and remembered that not too long ago she had helped him bring some wood in and start a fire in the fireplace. She continued with her list of ten different things. He thought for a while about each one of the things she listed. Not one of them required the expenditure of a lot of money. None of the things could be bought from a store. He realized how often we beat our heads against the wall trying to buy our children happiness, when in reality all his daughter was trying to say was: "Daddy, all I want is you!"

A third thing that Paul mentions is the father's responsibility for strengthening religion in their children. He admonishes fathers to bring up their children "in the discipline and instruction of the Lord." Again, it is interesting that he addresses this to fathers. Perhaps he was aware of the tendency among men to leave religious training to the mother. I heard about one father who took his responsibility seriously. He wanted his five-year-old son to be exposed to worship, and he wanted worship to be a positive experience. He and his wife always brought books and handwork to keep the child busy. One Sunday the boy just would not behave. He constantly talked and squirmed. The final straw came when his mother handed him a crayon, and he threw it across the sanctuary. His dad picked him up and tossed him across his shoulder and headed up the aisle. The father had his eyes fixed on the back doors, and the little fellow looked at the congregation over his father's shoulder. It was an obvious disturbance, and every eye followed them. Just as they reached the doors in the back of the church, the little fellow called in a loud, clear voice that everyone could hear, "Pray for me." At least, he had learned that assembled Christians pray.

Religious training also takes place at home. A Sunday school teacher asked the children seated in front of her, "Where is God's home?" The class was silent for a moment, then a little boy raised his hand. When the teacher asked him where God's home was, he answered confidently, "In the bathroom at my house!" "Why do you say that?" inquired the shocked teacher. He replied knowingly, "Because every morning my daddy bangs on the bathroom door and says, 'My Lord, are you still in there?' "

Religious instruction can be better than that. It is experienced in moments of warmth when the child knows he or she is loved. Frances Welsing, a Washington psychiatrist, says that the trouble with children is that they have too little "lap time." She is talking about an experience that we have all observed. A child wants to be held and the parent responds. After a while the child comes out of a state of deep relaxation and says, "Let me down." They've had enough. The problem, she says, is that too many of our children have too little "lap time." Welsing says she is constantly struck by how often, both in her clinical practice and in her frequent visits to schools, the answer comes back "no" when she asks teenagers if they got enough lap time when they were growing up. When children have those warm and intimate times with their parents, being read to, being held, being told a story, it is easier to believe in the benevolence of the God they learn to call Father.

Religious faith is something that is caught, more than it is taught. A misinformed father brought his son to church for religious instruction. After a while the boy protested against having to learn the catechism because he didn't understand it. The father answered him indignantly, "Who's expecting you to understand it — just learn it!" Too many people have been taught the faith just that way. They can describe some of the major beliefs, but they have never been given a vision of how the faith is lived. The Christian faith is caught in a Christian home.

Dr. William Farson, being quoted in a *Redbook* magazine article, said, "We have treated our children as if we could shape them the way a sculptor shapes clay. But that's not the way it is. It's more like we are running along and we fall on a pile of clay. We leave an impression all right, and that impression is distinctly us, but we have very little control over what it looks like. "You see," he continues, "in child raising, what parents are is terribly important. I suspect that kindness and decency, for instance, are learned by being around mothers and fathers who are kind and decent, and the same is true of other qualities."

We cannot make our children Christian, but we do influence them. Our children will ultimately decide for themselves what they will be, but that doesn't absolve parents of responsibility. Unfortunately, there are parents who say, with a certain amount of pride, that they do not intend to influence their children's decisions regarding religion. They will remain neutral and let the children choose for themselves. It sounds broadminded and rather democratic. But in point of fact, it is not possible to be religiously neutral. Religion is a spiritual atmosphere that pervades the entire home. We may decide not to coerce a child, but we certainly will influence, and if parents do not feel keenly enough about any faith to pass it on, it becomes apparent to the children that the parents don't have a faith worth mentioning.

A Christian home is a place where the ideals for living found in the life of Christ are accepted, exalted, and exemplified. It is a place where allegiance to Jesus Christ is woven into the fabric of the home. Here children can learn through simple prayers of thanks to acknowledge that God is with us wherever we are and that God is the sustainer of life. Of course, for the child to learn this, the parents need to be practicing it, and the earlier in their marriage a couple begins to practice, the more natural prayer will be for them. Parents can also introduce their children to some of the heroes of the faith by reading to them from a book of Bible stories. Parents are the principal teachers.

I close with this. Lola Falana, a well-known television personality a few years back, tells of a journey she had to make to what she calls "back home." "I had my own television specials," she says. "I'd become a success in a national commercial and I had headlined in Las Vegas. But in the wink of an eye it was all gone. I had a house on top of a mountain and in a closet I had built an altar. I didn't know then how much that altar would mean to me. One day I realized I had been leaning on the wrong arm, and I knelt at that altar and cried so hard my whole body shook. Then, suddenly, I felt a warm light all around me. I said, 'Please, God, I want to come home. Can I just come home to stay?' It was so simple. My mom and dad had taken me to Sunday school and had taught me about God and that helped me to make the journey for myself." We cannot make the journey of faith for our children, but we help them to find their home in God's universe when they see their parents express love for one another, when we take time to communicate with one another, and when, as

Paul says, we bring our children up "in the discipline and instruction of the Lord." In these ways, we give them a good foundation.

INDEPENDENCE DAY

God's Country
1 Peter 2:9-16

I have a friend who grew up in Arizona but spent his ministry serving churches in California. When he had a chance to return to Arizona, he took it readily, saying he was returning to God's country. I saw an advertisement for travel which said, "Come to gods' country." It attracted my attention because it was "gods" with a small "g" and a possessive plural. It turned out to be an invitation to come to Greece. I saw a fellow wearing a T-shirt that said, "I've been to God's country." He had been to Israel. There is a lot of that feeling in the Old Testament. Israel is frequently referred to as God's special people. There is little distinction between the nation as a political entity and as a people of faith.

In the first letter of Peter in the New Testament, Peter picks up this idea of a special people and applies it, not to a nation, but to the church. It occurred to me that as we make preparation to honor the birth of our nation, it would be useful for us to consider what a nation under God is called to be and how we, as Christian people, can help to make that calling a reality.

One of the things Peter says of the church is that at one time its members were "no people" but now they are "God's people." The term was first used in the Old Testament to remind Jews that at one time they were just a group of wandering nomads, but God had chosen them, called them to be a people, and in effect, put them on the map.

In some ways our own national heritage could be described that way. Certainly our own ancestors came from all over the world to settle here and make America what it is. On the street on which I grew up lived the Stakowskis from Poland, the Schreibers from Germany, the Alexanians from Armenia, the McDougals from Scotland, the Rognes from Norway, the De La Rues from France, the Cuthberts from England, the Enoss from Portugal, and the Wongs from China.

All of these were representatives of our country's character. On the great seal of the United States is the motto: *"E Pluribus Unum"*: "Out of many, one." People from everywhere, who by themselves were no people, have been welded into a great nation by a common aspiration: freedom. We come from people who have rallied around many flags, but we are bound together in loyalty to a new flag.

Perhaps this helps us to understand what Peter had in mind when he said of the church: "Once you were no people; now you are God's people." It isn't that we don't have other allegiances. We do, but when we choose individually to be God's people, those allegiances become secondary. A woman was telling me how moving it had been for her to attend a Rotary Convention in another country. There were representatives from 147 countries, each with their flag in evidence. But nationality was subservient to the ideals of Rotary, which brought them all together.

It occurred to me that she could have been speaking about the church. We who are part of the church may still identify with our race, profession, family, nation, the particular interests of our gender or our age group, but we recognize a higher allegiance to the God we have encountered in Jesus Christ, and that allegiance binds us together in spite of our special interests. Christ's banner over us is love, and in the parade that he leads, all our other flags have a secondary position.

When we were children in Sunday school, we were taught to sing: "Red and yellow, black and white, All are precious in his sight, Jesus loves the little children of the world."

That goes for the big children too, we might add. God's people are in every land; they come from every nation and race. Today, as we gather to receive communion from the table of our Lord, there are people of every nation doing the same thing. We are God's people, not by race, but by grace.

A second way Peter refers to the church is as "exiles and aliens." These, too, are familiar terms to those of us who make up this country. Exiles are people who have a home elsewhere, but for now they cannot go to it; they must live in a place which is not really their home.

Aliens are not always exiles, but often are thought of as people who are different from ourselves, people whose customs and language differ from our own, and perhaps people who are viewed with just a little suspicion because they are different. We *see* aliens, but few of us have had the experience of *being* aliens. My daughter lived in Japan for a couple of years. In her first letter to us she commented that from the moment she landed she had a different perspective of herself and how she fit into a new culture. The first door she had to go through at the airport was marked "alien," and that is what she felt she was during her entire stay.

Aliens are people who are not completely at home in their new land. They see things with which they disagree, things which residents do not even notice. Aliens may feel that they are only temporary residents; they still have ties with their homeland; they have traditions that they want to keep alive. So we see Cinco de Mayo celebrated in Mexican neighborhoods and Tet celebrations in Vietnamese neighborhoods. Most of our forebears came from somewhere else. Many of them settled in communities where they could keep their traditions alive, and for good or ill, they have had an impact on the culture of their host country.

This helps us to understand the meaning of these words as they are applied to the church. Once we have responded to the call to be God's people, this world is no longer our final destination. We have another homeland. We are aliens and exiles here. We may not respond to what other people respond to.

Henry David Thoreau said that if a person seems out of step with the crowd, perhaps it is because the person hears a different drummer. As Christians, let us be willing to be different; let us be content to be strange, to be conspicuous by our conduct if that is what it takes to do things differently from the world around us. We are here with temporary papers. We live in a world which, for the most part, does not recognize the sovereignty of God, but we do not have to agree with such a world.

Occasionally in our community I see men wearing long forelocks or black hats or black coats identifying them as Hasidic Jews. I see people dressed in white, wearing high turbans identifying them as Sikhs. Such people live among us but are not necessarily identified with our culture. Their different dress is a reminder to them and to us that they hear a different drummer. The world settles disputes by anger, revenge, violence, or power plays. As followers of the Prince of Peace let us determine that it will not be so with us. Let us live peaceably with one another acknowledging our differences but resolve, out of common loyalty to Jesus Christ, not to let our differences divide us. We are aliens, and it is appropriate that our style should be different from the style of those around us.

The third thing Peter says of Christians is that they should live as free people. What did he have in mind? For one thing, I think he meant that our new allegiance gives us freedom from the tyranny of things. An American tourist in Jerusalem met up with a Catholic monk. The monk offered to show the tourist around the monastery. When they came to the monk's room, the tourist noticed that there was no TV or radio, only one change of clothes, a towel, and one blanket. "Why do you live so simply?" asked the American. "Well," replied the monk, "I notice that you have only enough things to fill a suitcase. Why do you live so simply?" "I'm just a tourist," responded the American. "I'm only passing through." To which the monk replied, "So am I."

The world around us gauges worth by possessions. We who are called to live under God's rule must learn to see ourselves as trustees rather than owners, for nothing we have is ours to keep forever.

Another kind of freedom the Christian experiences is growing freedom from bondage to self. In Ibsen's play "Peer Gynt," the hero, consumed by his own self-centeredness, visits a lunatic asylum where, he assumes, he will find people who are outside themselves. The asylum director corrects him and points out that people in the asylum are not concerned about people outside themselves. They are completely turned in on themselves. They do not care for anyone besides themselves. They are imprisoned by self.

Ibsen was describing the bondage of every person who is the center of his own little universe. Freedom comes as one dethrones self and makes God the sovereign. When that happens, we are freed from self-centeredness and increasingly live in an expanded world made interesting by other people.

A third kind of freedom that Peter no doubt had in mind was the freedom that comes from experiencing grace. When we feel our acceptance is based on how good we are, we are in bondage to perfectionism. When we acknowledge that we are imperfect, we are freed from the tyranny of trying to be perfect. At the start of the 1988 baseball season, the Baltimore Orioles endured the worst start in history. They lost their first 23 games. While they were losing, they were big news. When they returned from a disastrous road trip in which they still hadn't won a game, 47,000 loyal fans filled the stadium in Baltimore. One of the Baltimore sportswriters suggested that in the good old days when the Orioles had been in contention for the World Series, there was tension in the air over every single game. But during the 1988 season the fans understood that the World Series was not an option, so they just came to have a good time. "If we win, that's okay. If not, you talk to your buddies and enjoy. Who cares?" The writer goes on to note that there is a certain freedom in a city where the team is in the cellar — a freedom to enjoy the sport for its own sake without the overload of the "we're number one" syndrome.

In a similar fashion, the freedom of the Christian comes from the experience of grace. When we realize that God's love is a gift and we don't have to earn it or deserve it, we don't have to strain to be accepted. We can be more relaxed and find enjoyment in the game God has given us to play.

Roy Angell, in his book *Shields of Brass*, tells about one of our ambassadors giving a speech: "You have invited me to tell you about the duties of an ambassador," he said. "Let me begin by telling you first of the embassy, the place where we live. The embassy is a little spot of America set down in an alien land. On the walls we have pictures of George Washington, Abraham Lincoln, Robert E. Lee, Stonewall Jackson, and the President of the United States, with a big flag — Old Glory — high over everything. When we had prohibition in the United States, we had prohibition in the embassy. Inside the embassy the laws of our own country are supreme. We celebrate Christmas, Thanksgiving, and the Fourth of July. Outside it is different. They celebrate none of these. Let me repeat, the embassy is a little spot of America in an alien land."

As Christians we are called to a style of life that will sometimes be at odds with the culture that surrounds us. This is as it should be, for we have declared our allegiance to another authority and that makes us aliens and exiles where we live. Let us do our best to see to it that our little spot becomes what it is supposed to be, an outpost of God's country.

LABOR DAY

More than Making a Living
Ecclesiastes 2:18-23; John 5:17

A father, exasperated with his son for not seeking work, says "Why don't you go out and get yourself a job?"

"Why?" asks the son.

"So you can earn some money."

"Why?"

"So you can put some money in the bank and earn interest."

"Why?"

"So that when you are old you can use the money in your bank account... and you'd never have to work again."

"But I'm not working now," responds the son, "so why should I go to work so I won't have to work?" Obviously, the father and son are not on the same wavelength.

Like many people, the son doesn't think too much of the idea of going to work. People commonly complain about the work they do. A Roper poll reported a few years ago that if people could live their lives over, 45% of those polled would pick a different career than the one they have. Obviously, they weren't satisfied with their work.

That was when jobs were plentiful. Today, there are hundreds of thousands of people who would be glad to have a job they dislike, just for the privilege of having a job.

A basic question for many people today is, "How are we going to survive?" Unemployment insurance is gone and those companies that have let people go are not hiring back.

Tony Garza's aerial mapping business, which he had been operating for 27 years folded in Ohio after government contracts dried up. Unable to find other work in Ohio, Tony and his wife Kay migrated to San Antonio and looked for work. A month later both were found fatally shot in the front seat of their car. Tony left bankruptcy papers, an empty wallet, a rifle, and a suicide note that said: "We've gone as far as we can with our lives. We are hard-working people who have been almost reduced to begging." Theirs is an extreme case, but none of us can discount the pain caused by lack of work.

Having acknowledged that, it is still the case that many who do have work don't enjoy it. And when the current economic situation improves, and work is once again available for those who are now unemployed, many of them will find that they are employed in an unsatisfying position. Since so much of our life is related to our employment, it occurred to me that on this Labor Sunday we would do well to consider the world of work.

The first thing we might do is to look at some reasons why work is an unsatisfying experience for many people. In a Labor Day speech some years ago, President Nixon said, "The work ethic holds that labor is good in itself; that a man or woman becomes a better person by virtue of the act of working. America's competitive spirit, the 'work ethic' of this people, is alive and well on this Labor Day." Yet, many people are less enthusiastic. They think of work as a curse.

Grace Clements is a felter in a luggage factory. She works in a tank six-feet deep and eight-feet square, molding pieces of wet felt in a hot press. Every forty seconds she forms a side of luggage. She runs 800 a day. "You are constantly moving and standing," she says. "If you talk during working you get a reprimand... we work eight straight hours, with two ten-minute breaks and one twenty minute break for lunch... you can't at any time leave the tank. In the summertime the temperature ranges anywhere from 100 to 150 degrees." For her there is no thought of work ethic, only survival.

It is no wonder that some people view the necessity of work as a curse. The idea that work is a curse goes all the way back to the writer of the story of Adam and Eve, for there sinful Adam hears the words: "In the sweat of your face you shall eat bread." When confronted with the hardship of making a living, some have found consolation in the idea that work is a curse put upon humans because of humanity's sin. But I wonder whether these words are to be read as a curse, placed upon labor to make it difficult, or whether this is a description of human attitudes toward work when humans have already alienated themselves from the source of fulfillment in life, which is God. When we lose sight of the image of God in ourselves or in those we employ, we are alienated from our destiny and it feels like a curse.

When a counselor at college tries to help a young person to decide on his life work, the process is called "Vocational Guidance." But when we talk about our daily work we may use the much less exalted word "job." The word "job" comes from an early English word meaning "lump." A job, then, is a shapeless, pointless, meaningless task that is set before us, and we are required to do it. This is precisely what the day's work has become for many men and women: a boring chore to be finished as quickly as possible. Daily work is a way to earn enough money to pay the bills and have enough leisure time left to get some fun out of life, since there is no fun involved from 8 am to 5 pm weekdays, as words like "rat race," "salt-mine," and "grind" indicate.

A number of things may contribute to the lump-like quality of our work. For one thing, our work may not give us a sense of fulfillment. Studs Terkel, an observer of the American scene, in his book *Working* interviewed hundreds of people to discover their attitudes toward work. Many complained of being dehumanized. "I'm just a machine," says the spot-welder in an automobile assembly plant. "I'm caged," says a bank teller. "I'm less than a farm implement," says a migrant worker. "They take care of the farm implements." "The machine dictates," says a receptionist. "This crummy little machine with buttons on it you've got to be there to answer it. You know you're not doing anything... for anyone. Your job doesn't mean anything because you are just a little machine. A monkey could do what I do." Indeed, some are dissatisfied because they feel dehumanized.

Others are dissatisfied because there is no sense of completion in their work. They want to contribute something that is uniquely theirs.

Mike Lefevre, a steelworker says: "I want my signature on (something). Sometimes, out of pure meanness, when I make something, I put a little dent in it. I like to do something to make it really unique. Hit it with a hammer... just so I can say I did it. It could be anything. I'd like to make my imprint... a mistake, mine. Let's say a whole building is nothing but red bricks. I'd like to have just one black one, or a white one or a purple one..." Most of us are looking for some way to leave our mark on something. Something that says, "I was here."

Still others are dissatisfied with their work because income has been the single most important consideration in choosing a position that in itself does not satisfy. Each of us is faced with the biological demand of staying alive, or perhaps in our day and age, of living reasonably well. The consideration of whether it will give expression to our spirit comes too late. A person may feel deeply destined to be an artist; but who can live on the income of most artists? There are not many clerks who can afford to leave their positions as did Paul Gaugin for a life of aesthetic abandon in the South Seas. Someone has said, "Hell is a job in which a person who needs to breathe air is forced to work underwater."

Having acknowledged that work is an unsatisfying experience for some, let us hasten to recognize that for many work is satisfying. In fact, Carl Michalson suggests that human beings are working animals whose very being is at stake in their handiwork. Unemployment contributes not only to our fear of starvation but to the frustration of our humanity.

I read about two American soldiers held as prisoners in Vietnam during the Vietnam War. One of their biggest complaints was that their captors would not let them do any work. They felt that the refusal to let them do anything creative was an intentional part of their treatment. When their captors finally allowed the prisoners to sweep their compound, it gave the men a sense of purpose that helped them to hold up their spirits. They came to value the opportunity to work.

The sources of this satisfaction appear to be quite varied. Some find that it comes from contributing to something enduring.

Carl Bates, a stonemason, is ecstatic about his work. "There's not a house in this county that I (have) built that I don't look at every time I go by," he says. "That's the work of my hands. 'Cause you see, you don't paint stone, you don't camouflage it. It's there, just like I left it forty years ago. It's something I can see the rest of my life." He feels he's been involved in something enduring.

For others, the satisfaction comes from making a contribution to people's needs. Tom Patrick, himself a New York fireman, tells of his pride in being a firefighter as he observed others fighting a fire while he was an off-duty bystander. "I see those fireman on the roof, with smoke pouring out around them, and the flames, and they go in. It fascinates me... that's what I do. The world's so (messed) up, the country's (messed) up. But you actually see the firemen put out a fire. You see them come out with babies in their hands. You see them give mouth-to-mouth when a guy's dying. You can't get around that... That's real. That's what I want to do."

For still others, their satisfaction comes from serving and serving well. Dolores Dante has been a waitress in the same restaurant for 23 years. "I get intoxicated with giving service," she says, "Some waitresses don't care. When the plate is put down you can hear the sound. I try not to have that sound. I want my hands to be right when I serve. I pick up a glass, I want it to be just right... I like it to look nice all the way. To be a waitress, it's an art. I feel like a ballerina too. I have to go between those tables, between those chairs...I know they can see how delicately I do it. I'm on stage... When somebody says to me, 'You're great, how come you're just a waitress?' I say, 'Just a waitress!' I say, 'Why, don't you think you deserve to be served by me?' I don't feel lowly at all. I don't want to change my job. I love it."

Perhaps the sources of satisfaction are not as varied as we first imagined. Perhaps satisfaction in our work is not something that we derive from it, but something that we bring to it. Perhaps not all work can be rewarding, but socially necessary work serves human need. Our work may not give us significance, but we can give it significance if we know who we are, and our work becomes an expression of who we are.

The third thing I want to suggest is that, for many, their work, whatever it is, takes on meaning when they see themselves in partnership with God. Far from being a result of sin, work began with and is a continuing activity of God. As children, we are apt to see God as just sitting there, ruling. But Jesus said, "My Father is working still, and I am working" (John 5:17). When we see God with his sleeves rolled up working for a better world, we begin to understand the true nature of God much better. God is still in business, creating a world. God may have rested on the Sabbath day, but God didn't quit.

The universe is incomplete, it is still in the process of being created. There are still diseases to be overcome. There are human emotions to be tamed. There are resources to be uncovered; principles to be put into practice. God is working still.

The Bible also states repeatedly that God ordained work for us. In the creation account, our forebears are told to subdue the earth and have dominion over it. Therefore, tasks, humble and exalted, fall to us. God has chosen us to be co-creators with him in finishing his creation, partners in the task of building all people into community. Junior partners, perhaps, but not employees, for we are called to work "with" God not simply "for" God. We make some of the decisions; we share in the responsibility. Let us not feel that work is a curse and beneath our dignity, for God is working and it is not beneath the dignity of God.

The biblical word for this idea of partnership is "vocation." It means quite simply, "calling." Originally the calling was thought to be from God to perform certain tasks. We still refer to some professions as callings, but the restricted use of the word in our time indicates the extent to which our culture has lost the sense of vocation.

We have allowed "the call" to become almost exclusively the property of those entering occupations in the field of religion. In the church in which I grew up the preacher often gave the invitation to enter "full-time Christian service," which in that context meant becoming a preacher or a missionary. A lot of people responded who might have done better at something else.

I heard a story about a devout farm boy looking skyward one day who saw the clouds hazily form the three letters "G P C" and concluded it to be a message from God — "Go Preach Christ." He left his secular employment to pursue that vocation but failed miserably. After hearing him tell the story of his "calling" in a rather abysmal sermon, a layperson took him aside and suggested that he had misinterpreted the sign, that the "G P C" probably meant "Go Plow Corn."

Our calling comes from God. We are all called to be partners. Being a religious professional is not the only way to answer the call.

John Rich once pointed out that if everybody spent their time contemplating the infinite instead of doing plumbing, many of us would die of cholera. God's call consists in God's summoning persons to live and serve in obedience to his will and in fulfillment of his purpose for the world.

Such an understanding of God's calling provides for great diversity of function. The task of all persons is to subdue the earth — that is, to bring everything into subjection to the will of God.

The engineer is not taming the impersonal forces of nature, but bringing some part of the earth into subjection to the ultimate purpose of God. The diplomat is not simply serving her country, she has the possibility of creating understanding between peoples who might otherwise remain alienated. The builder is not in business simply to enlarge profits by cutting corners, but rather to provide a wholesome setting in which families may grow. The homemaker has opportunity to create a nurturing environment in which human bodies can grow and mature, a place where ingredients can be put together to create tasty and nutritious meals. If an occupation is a necessary one and serves a purpose, then it has meaning and it justifies a person doing it, for God has called us to carry out our Christian concern in whatever ways are open to us. Those who respond to the call to work with God will find that their work is thereby given meaning. Let us acknowledge that not all work is equally creative. If we are involved in an occupation that seems to allow only limited creativity, then let us seek out those opportunities naturally associated with the work, through which a sense of fulfillment may be gained: perhaps sympathetic listening to an associate, counseling a fellow worker, active participation in the labor union, or in the redeeming of the office Christmas party. Only when we see our daily work as vocation — calling from God — do we have a sound basis for making the decisions that must be made about our daily work.

Only when we understand that God has called us to fill a particular place in the fulfillment of God's purpose are we in a position to see how we are responsible for others and how our actions significantly influence the lives of those about us. We do not all search for a cancer cure, teach the ignorant, or fight the fires that threaten us, but if our work is useful and we do it well, we provide the kind of community in which others are freed to do these things, and our work is made meaningful because we have contributed to the outcome.

Anthony Campolo, while visiting Scotland with his wife, wanted to visit the shipyards where her grandfather had worked before the family immigrated to America. They asked directions of a middle-aged woman who informed them that she was at that very moment on her way to her job at the shipyard and would be glad to take them there personally. Campolo writes, "On our way we passed numerous shipbuilders who had just finished their work on the daytime shift. Each of them bid an enthusiastic greeting to our new friend. Everybody we passed knew her by name and she, likewise, knew everyone we encountered. There was a fun-loving quality about her personality, and her whole demeanor communicated that she was enjoying life. 'What's your job at the shipyard?' I asked. She stopped in her tracks, took my arm, and then spoke to me in such a way that I was sure she was about to tell me something of enormous importance. 'What do I do?' she asked rhetorically. 'What do I do? I'm the one who cleans the ships.' And then, obviously impressed with the importance of her task, she added, 'And you know, nary a ship goes to sea until I say it's clean enough. It's my job to see to it that every bit of dirt is polished away. That's what I do.' "

There was a person who saw how her work contributed to the whole. She brought significance to her work, her work took on meaning, and as a result she was involved in far more than making a living. She was investing a life.

STEWARDSHIP SUNDAY

Increasing the Joy
2 Corinthians 8:1-15

A young girl approached a thrifty Scotsman, asking him to contribute to a charity. "Give until it hurts," she said. "Oh, lassie," he replied, "if you knew how painful it is just to *think* about it, you wouldn't even ask."

For many of us, the idea of joyful giving is an oxymoron. And yet the Bible talks about it. In Paul's second letter to the Christians at Corinth, he speaks of some people in another part of Greece who gave out of the abundance of their joy.

When Paul set out on his missionary journeys, he was asked by the apostles to take up an offering for the poor Christians in Jerusalem wherever he established a church in the West. He had proposed such an offering to the Corinthian congregation when he was among them, and they had begun to collect it. In the meantime, however, he had had to write to them critically about their conduct, and this had created hard feelings. The hard feelings had eventually been addressed and overcome, and he was now looking for a delicate way to bring up the subject once again. As he does so, he lays out some principles for joyous giving that would be well for us to consider so that we don't wind up like the thrifty Scotsman.

The first thing he talks about in giving is motive. God knows that some of the motivation for giving promoted by the church has been questionable. There has been the appeal of promised rewards. "If you tithe, you'll be blessed." I frankly believe that. But in some instances that statement has degenerated to "if you tithe, God will benefit you materially." People who begin to tithe on the assumption that God will give then a raise or pay their debts are looking for magic — not religion.

Apparently that motivation still goes on today. An embittered man sued God for $800 in back tithes. The charge was that God did not deliver on a Miami, Florida, pastor's promise that "blessings and awards would come to the person" who gave 10% of his income to his church. When neither blessing nor award surfaced after a three-year waiting period, the 47-year-old plumber decided to "invest" his money elsewhere. He went to court to get back his money. The last I heard was that the court agreed with the plaintiff and decided that God should return the money, but God had not appeared to answer the judgment.

It was that teaching of promised reward that broke Luther's patience with the church and brought on the Reformation. The church needed money and authorized the sale of indulgences: blanket forgiveness without repentance. "As soon as the coin in the casket rings, the soul from Purgatory springs," cried the promoter. What a sham this made of decent Christianity. It suggested that righteousness could be bought and sold. Some people still have that impression today.

Another questionable motive has been an appeal to fear. "You reap what you sow," we are told. I believe that too, but I don't think you can place Christian stewardship on a "you'd better give, or else" basis. Even if people do part with their resources in fear, they have not exercised stewardship. A colleague told me about a woman in his church who was near death. She felt her life hadn't been all it should have been and she wanted to set things right. She called the minister to her home and indicated that she wanted to give the church $70,000. The minister thanked her and prayed with her. Two weeks later her health was much improved, and she indicated that she had changed her mind. Evidently, her fears regarding the hereafter had subsided.

The *Annual Review of Psychology* reported on a study that concluded that churchgoers are less likely to contribute to a charitable cause following confession and absolution than prior to it. They apparently feel less need to placate God.

We need better motives for giving than that. One that Paul alludes to is gratitude. The Macedonian Christians begged Paul for the opportunity to contribute to the offering he was taking. There was no need to cajole them, he says. They wanted to participate out of gratitude. The Christian writer, Jim Bishop, began to write down the things for which he was grateful, and his list turned into a prayer: "Oh Lord, I thank you for the privilege and gift of living in a world filled with beauty and excitement and variety. I thank you for the gift of loving and being loved, for the friendliness and understanding and beauty of the animals on the farm and in the forest and marshes, for the green of the trees, and sound of a waterfall, the darting beauty of the trout in the brook. I thank you for the delights of music and children, for the beauties of the four seasons... for the powers of the mind... for all the senses you have bestowed upon me and for the delights which they bring me. I thank you for the smile on the face of a woman, the touch of a friend's hand, for the laughter of a child, the wagging tail of a dog and the touch of his cold nose against my face... Thank you, God, for life itself, without which the universe would have no meaning." We may not have Bishop's capacity to create verbal images, but when we allow ourselves to reflect on the blessings we have received, it leads to gratitude that makes us want to share.

Another appropriate motive for giving is the sense of stewardship — an awareness that we are trustees of what has been put into our hands. One fellow urges us to think of stewardship as driving a leased car. You can do what you want with the car, but when the time comes for it to be returned to the owner, the user will be held accountable for the condition in which it is returned. Paul reminds the Corinthians that they have been blessed with abundance in order that they may make up for what others lack. What they have has not been given for their benefit alone but for the benefit of others.

Not only do we need a proper motive if our giving is going to promote joy, we need a proper measurement of our giving. One inadequate measurement for our giving is the budget of an organization. Each year about this time the finance committee of the church puts together a projected budget for the coming year and distributes that information to the congregation. This year we are not going to do that, because it focuses on the church's need to receive rather than the giver's need to give. One is subtly encouraged to divide the amount needed by the number of members to come up with a "fair share." Considering the differences in our resources, "fair share" may be a burden for some and a token for others. In either case it doesn't promote joy in giving.

Another inadequate measurement is the actions of others. I have seen pledge cards that say, "In consideration of the gifts of others, I will give so much to my church." That is simply keeping up with one's neighbors. It is asking the question, "How much do I have to give to be acceptable to those around me?" I heard about one church that listed the number of pledges at each giving level. One fellow had made a substantial pledge and could see how far ahead of others his pledge was. He became incensed because he felt others were doing too little, and he withdrew his support altogether. Not much joy in giving there.

Let the measurement be sacrificial giving, says Paul. He mentions the sacrifice of the Macedonians who contributed out of their poverty. Because they were poor, they knew what poverty was and they reached out to others. Consider Christ, he says, who gave himself so we might know God's love.

I was talking with a girl who is an exchange student from Peru. She loves the United States and has been helped by the generosity of its people. However, she noted a difference in the way our respective people give. She says she feels that in America when we give something we say in effect, "Here, you take this, I don't really need it." Whereas, in her homeland, when people give out of their poverty, they are understood to be saying, "I could use this, but I want you to have it." When a gift is made sacrificially, it means so much more to giver and receiver.

What Paul is calling for is generosity. When we don't share out of our abundance, what we have to share begins to get stale. I learned that when I was away at college. My girlfriend sent me a big box of brownies she had made. I knew that if my roommates got wind of it, the brownies would be gone in a flash. So I put them in a dresser drawer, taking a nibble when no one else was around, which was seldom. Several weeks later we had a party, and I thought I would finally break out the brownies. But by that time they had become rancid, stale, and dry. "That's what you get for not sharing when you should have," said one of the roommates, and he was right.

A Navajo American tells about his brother who is a hotshot

bronco rider. "He's won several big prizes," says the brother, "but he's going to start losing because he's been keeping his winnings." The Navajo went on to explain: "In our culture, if you have a lot of money and material goods when people around you are without, it puts you out of harmony. It's taken for granted among Navajos that if you have a lot of money you're not a good person, because if you're a Navajo, you've got poor relatives, and you should be sharing." That's a statement Christians should ponder carefully.

Not only do our motivation and our measurement need to be appropriate if our giving is to bring joy, so does our method. We need to learn to give proportionally. Paul advises the Corinthians to give according to what they have, not according to what they don't have. Unfortunately, as a people, the more we make, the less we give. In a report on giving trends, it was noted that those who had incomes of less than $10,000 gave an average of 5.5% to charity. Those making more than $100,000 gave only 2.9%.

This is why the church has historically encouraged tithing. A tithe is 10% of one's income. Some people reject the idea of tithing. They say that it makes Christian giving too legalistic. A pastor had just finished preaching about God's free gift of salvation. He compared it to the free gifts of sunshine, air, and water. Then, following a short prayer, he gave an appeal to his congregation to improve their record of giving. Following the service, one of the members of the congregation took issue with the appeal to improve giving. "I thought you said salvation is free," scolded the member. The pastor thought for a moment and then answered, "Indeed it is free, but we have to pipe it to the people who need it, and somebody has to pay for the plumbing."

A number of members in a congregation I served took the challenge seriously a few years ago, and they embarked on a program to make that church a tithing church by a set date. They developed a banner that said "A Promise to Fulfill," and they lighted a tithing lamp each Sunday to remind themselves of that goal. Many people have committed to the challenge by adding 1% of their income each year to their giving. They are growing in their experience of the joy connected with giving. I saw a bumper sticker that says "Honk if you love Jesus." But there is one I like better. It says, "If you love Jesus, tithe; anyone can honk."

Paul also reminds us that if our giving is going to bring joy, it has to be purposeful. Several years ago a popular Dallas Deejay, Ron Chapman, reminded his listeners to get their twenty dollars in as soon as possible. He didn't say what it was for. He just wanted to see what people would do. Days later Chapman had received $244,000 from 12,212 listeners. He subsequently had to ask his listeners for ideas on how to spend the money. That may be giving, but it doesn't reflect any sense of responsibility. It is not stewardship. It is not expressive of purpose.

Paul, on the other hand, urges the Christians at Corinth to be responsible in their giving. He invites them to give through their church to meet the needs of the poor in a distant city. One of the ways we experience joy in our giving is to give intentionally, to know where the gift is going, so we can rejoice in what is being accomplished.

Important as appropriate motivation, appropriate measurement, and appropriate method are for joyous giving, there is something that precedes all these considerations. It is personal commitment. Paul says of those Macedonians, "first they gave themselves." In the final analysis, our self is the only thing we really have to give, and if we are to have any joy in our giving, our self is the first thing to give. One Christian has said, "Stewardship is what I do after I have said I believe." First we have to enlist in the cause, which is to extend God's work in the world. After that, our efforts to advance the cause contribute to the joy.

WORLD COMMUNION SUNDAY

Communion by the Sea
John 6:5-15, 25-35

Introduction to the Service

Today our order of worship will be altered in a way that we hope will help all of us to experience and better appreciate a biblical event. Instead of a sermon in a specific place, the unfolding activities of the biblical event will be recounted and expanded upon at various points during the service. First, let us become familiar with the biblical account of what happened as the scripture is read.

John 6:5-15, 25-35 is read.

The Gathering

The people were coming together to listen. There was anticipation in their minds as to what they might hear. Let us gather up our thoughts and expectations for the time we shall spend together in this service of worship. To prepare ourselves, in a moment we will stand to join our voices in singing the hymn "We Gather Together."

The Setting

It was perhaps the second year of Jesus' ministry. Jesus was at the height of his popularity. It was in the spring, just before the Jewish Festival of Passover. Many people were on their way from Galilee and points north to Jerusalem so that they might be in the Holy City for the celebration. As they passed through Galilee they heard that the popular teacher, Jesus of Nazareth, was in the vicinity preaching and healing the sick. So it was that many turned aside to go and see and hear for themselves. This took them off the beaten path out to a hill overlooking the Sea of Galilee. There Jesus did indeed speak to them, so they lingered longer than they should have. Many of them had undoubtedly become hungry, but they were far away from a town where they could purchase food.

Realizing their dilemma, Jesus turned to one of his disciples, Philip, and asked, "How are we to buy bread so that all these people can eat?" It was logical that he should ask Philip, for they were in Philip's territory, but when Philip heard the question he almost choked. This was no family outing; it wasn't a little picnic in the park. To feed this number of people would call for an airlift. There were well over 5,000 people there. Just a little lox and bagels and a dash of potato salad for each one present would set somebody back six months' wages. Philip knew that Judas carried the bankroll for their operation and he wasn't having any trouble carrying all of it in a very small bag. They couldn't afford to feed all these freeloaders, and besides, there weren't enough kosher delicatessens in the whole region to take on the job. Like many of us, Philip was a realist. "The problem is unmanageable, Jesus. Just dismiss the crowd and let them fend for themselves." There was no hopefulness in Philip, no imagination, no new ideas.

Andrew, Simon Peter's brother, was standing nearby. He couldn't help but overhear the conversation. In fact, the rumblings in his own stomach had told him sometime earlier that he had better be on the lookout for somebody with a large lunch. As luck would have it, he found a little boy who had cut school to go fishing. The boy had seen the crowd gathering to listen to Jesus, and since this was the biggest thing to hit these parts in years, he decided to postpone the fishing in favor of the medicine show. The boy managed to stash away some lox and bagels from breakfast and it was the pleasing aroma of these things that had attracted Andrew's attention. When Andrew indicated how good it smelled, the boy freely offered to share his lunch with Andrew. Andrew's needs, at least, were going to be met. Now that Jesus was pointing out that everyone was hungry, Andrew was smitten in conscience and sheepishly announced that he had found a boy who was willing to share his lunch. But it wouldn't do much good, Andrew was quick to point out, if Jesus intended to share it with everyone.

Surprisingly, Jesus responded to this offer as a concrete beginning to the solution of the problem. Instead of being immobilized by the enormity of the problem, here was someone willing to respond with the little that he had. One doesn't have to do everything before one can begin to do something. What resources do we have, inadequate as they may seem to be, which can be placed at God's disposal in helping to meet the enormous human problems that surround us today?

In a moment we will stand to sing our second hymn of the morning as the elements of our communion are brought forward.

The Serving

Jesus took the bread and the fish, offered a prayer of thanksgiving over it, and gave it to his disciples to distribute. John, one of the disciples, was there that day. What subsequently happened had such a profound impact on him that as he later recorded the incident he did so in great detail. However, John did not get around to writing down his version of the story of Jesus until long after the death of Jesus. By that time there were already a number of congregations meeting regularly in the name of Jesus, breaking bread and drinking wine in memory of Jesus.

All the gospel writers recall that Jesus gathered his disciples together on his last night to share a Passover meal. Three of them recall the words of institution: "As often as you eat this bread and drink this cup, do it in remembrance of me." But not John. As far as John is concerned, the Lord's supper had already been instituted in another Passover occasion beside the Sea of Galilee. In the catacombs, those underground Christian burial places where early Christians met, the symbols that are still visible on the walls show loaves and fishes for the communion meal, rather than bread and wine. Even as John wrote these words, the initiated Christian was invited to see beyond the description of a mysterious meal by the sea and to recognize that John was talking about the sacrament of communion.

It is that sacrament that we propose to experience here today. We have the bread, which reminds us of the Body of Christ broken for us. We have the fruit of the vine, rather than the fish, for the juice reminds us more graphically of the blood that Jesus shed as he sought to express the nature of sacrificial love. We have here such persons as Jesus invited to distribute the elements so long ago. And we have here the people whom Jesus, in his compassion, invited to partake of these elements. All who wish to join us in partaking of these elements are invited to do so, regardless of age or church affiliation, so long as they desire to live a new life in Jesus Christ.

In a moment the ushers will guide us forward to receive the elements from any of the people at the front of the church. Take a piece of bread, dip it in the cup, partake of it, and return to your seat. Any who would like to commune, but who are unable to come forward, are requested to make that known to an usher. They will be served in their seats. Any who do not wish to commune may simply remain in their seats. First, however, let us join our voices in the communion prayer, even as Jesus prayed before he distributed the elements.

The Gathering In

What actually happened that day by the sea we shall never know for sure. By the time John wrote down his description of the incident it had been lovingly told hundreds of times in the young church and perhaps to emphasize different points. Even today, interpretations differ. Many simply attribute the feeding of so many to a miracle, and if one is satisfied to focus on the miraculous, then let that explanation suffice. Others see it as a description of a sacramental meal such as our communion meal was this morning — each person receiving a small morsel. And since John does not mention the last supper elsewhere, it would appear that he saw this event as of sacramental significance. Still others feel that by offering to share the small boy's lunch, Jesus stimulated others to share, who had previously been afraid to share what they had with them lest there not be enough for themselves. If this is what happened, it means that human beings who had been afraid to share were changed into human beings who were ready to give, and the miracle becomes not the miracle of changing little food into much food but the miracle of changing selfish people into sharing people.

However it was accomplished, when all had eaten and were satisfied, Jesus told his disciples to go among the people and gather up the fragments. There was enough left so that each disciple collected a basketful. The baskets mentioned were like lunch pails that Jews carried with them when they traveled so that they would have kosher food even though they might be among Gentiles. The significance of the gathering up is that there was enough left over, after feeding the multitude, to take care of those who did the serving.

Today there are people who are serving in the name of Jesus Christ all around the world: in this community, the ghetto, the jungle, the bush country, the reservation, everywhere. Their ability to continue to serve is dependent upon our capacity to share. As on that day by the sea so long ago, there are those who are ready to pass among us to receive what we have to share. Let us be generous.

The Misunderstanding of the Sign

To say the least, some in the crowd were pretty impressed by what had taken place. Those on welfare found this better than food stamps. If they could just stay close to Jesus they wouldn't have to bother with all that government red tape. The religious people could see benefits here too: all those food banks that are so hard to fill; all those boxes of groceries to help the unemployed. And the incident was not lost on the hot-blooded young nationalists who saw in Jesus' trick the possibility of feeding a revolutionary army when they were ready to make their bid for power. It didn't take any effort at all to get the crowd to start singing "For He's A Jolly Good Fellow" and chanting slogans such as "Jesus for President." This was not the kind of notoriety Jesus had in mind, however, and while people were working out still other cheers, Jesus slipped away to be by himself.

Those with big plans for Jesus' future were not easily discouraged, however. The next day a number of them tracked Jesus to the other side of the lake and began to ask him questions. But Jesus saw through their intentions. They were not attracted by his message; he just happened to be someone they could use to further their own plans. They wanted to sign Jesus up for what they could get out of him. They had witnessed what had happened, but they did not see it as a sign of anything. Jesus tried to set them straight: "You have come looking for me simply because your stomachs were filled, and not because you really understood what was going on," he said.

In those words Jesus put his finger on a problem that still troubles those who seek to follow him. Each of us has our own list of things we hope to receive: success in business, success in romance, peace of mind, safety for ourselves or loved ones, escape from some dreaded problem. And there is nothing wrong with such requests. Often they emanate from love. In any case, they are an acknowledgment that we are weak and limited children who can do little more than ask for help. The problem is that we are often willing to *remain* as children when what we need to do is to help solve problems by saying to God such things as "make me," "mold me," "use me," "show me." Bread is essential to life, and we are taught to ask for it, but there is more to life than just bread.

The Meaning of the Sign

It is in Jesus' words that we find the meaning of the sign. "Do not spend all your efforts for the food that spoils," said Jesus, "but for that which endures to eternal life." Jesus had caught their attention by meeting a physical need, but he hoped that they would move on from preoccupation with food to more ultimate questions such as, "What are we to do with these lives that are sustained by God's gifts?" Fortunately that question did occur to someone, because someone from the back of the crowd, wearied by all the double-talk, eventually asked Jesus flat out, "All right, what *should* we be doing, to be doing what God wants us to do?"

Jesus answered, "What God wants you to do is to believe in the one whom he has sent." Now Jesus was becoming too specific. It was all right to think of him as some kind of miracle worker who could expand food, but for Jesus to suggest that this was evidence that he was sent from God was a little bit much. Nevertheless, this was the connection Jesus was hoping that they would make.

One of the more religious people in the crowd began to see a connection with an incident out of their past, for he said, in effect, "If you want us to believe in you, you are going to have to do better than you've done so far, Jesus. In the old days our people were hungry while in the wilderness and Moses fed them with manna, that strange food from heaven, for forty years. Obviously, Moses was from God, but you, you fed us once. What else can you do to convince us so that we can believe?" Jesus then responded, "I not only give the bread of life, I *am* the bread of life."

Here, then, was the significance of the act of feeding the previous day: though that bread had sustained the physical body temporarily, the nourishment it offered was short-lived. In our communion service today the food that was provided, while real enough, was also little enough so that we would not fall into the trap of seeing it as just another meal. It stands for something beyond itself. It is a sign pointing to someone who can nourish our spirits: Jesus Christ. As those physical elements are taken into our bodies and literally turned into energy, we are being reminded that there is a bread of life who feeds our souls, who energizes us, who empowers us to continue his ministry in the world. "I am the bread of life," says Jesus, "The one who comes to me shall not hunger, and the one who believes in me shall never thirst."

REFORMATION DAY

Great Scot! John Knox
Malachi 3:1-4

I have never felt that God intended for women to rule. My life became difficult when I made those thoughts public. Some time about mid-life, I wrote a pamphlet titled "The Monstrous Regiment of Women," the purpose of which was to show the woes that have come upon the race through the reign of women. As you will see presently, my own experiences have corroborated my views. At the same time, my pamphlet made it even more difficult to deal with these women rulers.

The issues I want to speak about are, of course, much deeper than my feelings about women rulers. The issues concern freedom of religion, freedom from foreign domination, freedom of conscience, and freedom from corruption in the church. Those of us who had these convictions were called Reformers, though we also saw ourselves as patriots. My name is John Knox, one-time priest of the Roman Catholic Church in Scotland, but more recently, an opposer of that church as God chose to use my efforts to establish the Protestant church in Scotland.

Let me tell you something about my early life so that you will have a better appreciation for why things happened as they did in Scotland.

I was born near Huntington in the year 1513. Luther had not yet issued his challenge to the church in Germany. That came four years later. In 1527, a Scotsman by the name of Patrick Hamilton, who had been studying on the continent, came home and began to preach some of the doctrines that were being proclaimed by the Reformers. Hamilton was summoned to trial, found guilty of heresy, and burned at the stake. As he stood bound to the stake, he prayed that God would open the eyes of his fellow citizens. When he was unable to speak any longer, he held up his fist as a token of steadfast faith.

People eventually began to ask why he had been burned. I was only fourteen years of age at the time, but his death made an impression on me.

Nevertheless, I continued my education at Saint Andrews University in preparation for entering the priesthood of the Roman church. At the age of 27 I was ordained as a priest. I had some misgivings about what was going on in Scotland, but my teachers urged me to revere the teachings of the Catholic church and to be loyal to Scotland, for anyone who embraced the Reformed church might give comfort to Henry VIII in England, who was looking for ways to gain control over Scotland.

When our king died in 1542, his infant daughter, Mary Stuart, came to the throne. A Regent was appointed, who was sympathetic to the Protestant cause, and he caused the infant Queen to become engaged to the English Prince, Edward VI.

About that time, another Scotsman, George Wizard, returned from the continent teaching the Reformed faith. He taught that the Bible was supreme over the councils of men; we are saved by faith, not by our good work; all believers are priests of God; many of the rites and ceremonies of the church are simply superstition and should be done away with. I heard him gladly and I became a close associate of his. In 1543 he was arrested. He was tried and burned at the stake in 1546. As the flames engulfed him, he forgave those who condemned him. I also became suspect because I had been a close associate of his.

A new Regent who opposed all Reformed thought had come to power, and friends urged me to flee to Saint Andrew's Castle where there was a garrison of people who were sympathetic to Reformed doctrine. I went there and before long the occupants asked me to become their preacher, though I was still a Roman priest. In this setting, I began to express myself about some of the errors in the Catholic church that I felt needed correction. A number of the people in the town professed the Reformed faith. Soon what had only been a Protestant sentiment within the Roman church became a church in its own right. The Catholic archbishop was alarmed and through his political connections he arranged for 21 French ships, assisted by the Scottish army, to surround the town.

After a siege of one month, an agreement was reached whereby the lives of the defenders of the castle would be spared. We were to be transported to France and from there to any country of our choosing, except Scotland. We surrendered and we were sent to France, but the terms of the agreement were not kept! Every one of us was imprisoned in France or sent to be galley slaves on French ships. I was one of the latter. For nineteen months I was chained by the neck, bound to a bench in the hold of a ship, sometimes obliged to row for twelve hours a day without interruption, lashed by whips, given scant food, clothing, or shelter. All the while I was being advised that if I would renounce my Protestant views, I would immediately be released. God gave me the grace to endure. Others could not, and they gave up. Eventually, the French, English, and Scottish governments negotiated a prisoner exchange, and I was released.

By now, of course, I was committed to the Protestant cause. I could not return to Scotland where the court was ardently Roman Catholic, so I settled in England. The English church was becoming more and more reformed and many of the abuses of Roman Catholicism were being rooted out. The Scots, however, distrusted the political intentions of the English and therefore were fearful of Protestantism. Instead, they gravitated toward Catholic France as an ally. Mary Stuart's engagement to the English prince was broken, and she was engaged instead to the French heir apparent, the Dauphin. I was assigned to minister in a border town where people were half-Scot and half-English. I proclaimed Reformed doctrine, spoke out against the mass and superstitious rites, and urged discipline upon the loose-living inhabitants of that border town. Before long, I was asked to become pastor in a larger town. I was made a royal chaplain and eventually offered the office of Bishop of Rochester. I declined the latter, for I felt that it would prevent me from ever serving my own country, Scotland. In 1553 the young English king died and his sister the Roman Catholic Mary Tudor acceded to the English throne. English royal favor was withdrawn from the Reformation movement. I lost my pastorate, the royal chaplaincy was removed, and my mail was being intercepted. It was apparent that my arrest was imminent. Friends urged me to escape, which I did. I settled in Switzerland. It was there that I came under the friendship and the tutelage of the great Swiss reformers, Calvin, Beza, and Zwingli. They helped me greatly to think through Reformed doctrine and its implications for Scotland.

At this time, several questions were developing in my mind, which would have implications for all of Europe. Chief among them was the question: Is it proper to have female rulers, who may transfer the governance of their realms to their foreign husbands? Mary Tudor in England was about to marry a Catholic fanatic, Philip of Spain, and Mary Stuart of Scotland was about to marry the Catholic French Dauphin. To ask such a question was to challenge the notion of the divine right of monarchs to rule. They were theological questions too for scripture urges us to be submissive to those in authority. Out of questioning came my pamphlet on "The Monstrous Regiment of Women," which you can understand was not well received in either Scotland or England. Further, I was perceived to be an anarchist, for I wrote to my afflicted friends in England, suggesting to them that not all statutes of law are necessarily legal and not everything that ungodly people may call treason is necessarily a sin. I suggested that sometimes one may need to act against the law out of conscience. I stayed on in Geneva becoming pastor of a congregation of Protestant English-speaking refugees who were living there.

In the British Isles, government was in the control of women, and things were going badly for Protestants. In England, Mary Tudor had married the Spanish prince and was persecuting Protestants, arresting, exiling, and killing fine churchmen. For this, she became known as "Bloody Mary." In Scotland, Mary Stuart had married the French prince and was living in France, while her mother ruled as regent in Scotland. The Scottish Protestant nobles urged me to visit Scotland, for they hoped that I could strengthen the church. I did go and spent my time evangelizing in the countryside and urging Protestants to celebrate the Lord's Supper rather than to participate in the Roman mass. Because of my success in persuading Protestants not to attend mass, which we felt to be idolatrous, I was called to trial for heresy by the Catholic hierarchy. I appeared but the trial was called off, and the Protestants appeared to have won the right to have a church of their own.

I was called back to my congregation in Geneva, but before I left I urged the Scottish Protestants to meet weekly, even when they did not have clergy so that they might worship and discuss scripture. The Scottish Protestant church was on its way to becoming an organization in which laypeople would have an increasing voice.

About this time, the Catholic Queen of England died and the Protestant Elizabeth was coming to the throne. The Scottish Regent felt that she had better strengthen Scotland against this Protestant influence, so she had the Privy Council prohibit preaching by unauthorized people, meaning Protestants.

The Protestant nobles in Scotland again called on me to come back to my homeland, this time permanently. I said farewell to my congregation in Geneva and set out for Scotland.

When I arrived in Scotland in 1559, numerous Protestant preachers had been cited for unauthorized preaching and were to stand trial. I decided to stand with them. Protestant laypeople were preparing for a show of support, so the Regent was prevailed upon to call off the trial in order to avoid civil unrest. When the people had dispersed, the Regent accused the preachers of failing to appear, pronounced us to be outlaws and rebels, and proclaimed that the movement was to be crushed. She raised an army in an effort to suppress Protestants. Mobs began sweeping through churches, breaking windows, and throwing down idols. We clergy insisted that we did not encourage such behavior. All we wanted was the freedom to worship as we saw fit. The Regent would not listen.

Once again the Protestant forces sought protection in the castle of Saint Andrews. The Regent and her army surrounded us there, insisting that our call for religious reform was simply a cloak to cover political rebellion. The Regent was hoping for French troops to strengthen her army, while we Protestants were hoping for English troops to reinforce us. For this reason, the Regent allowed the Protestant army to leave Edinburgh, with an agreement that there would be no conflict for six months.

Following the cessation of hostilities, I was invited by the congregation at Saint Giles Church in Edinburgh to become its first Protestant pastor. I accepted the position but almost at once I was called upon by the Protestant movement to seek the help of England in our cause. Eventually this was forthcoming and when the battle was engaged, it was really a battle between French and English forces, assisted on both sides by Scots. The Regent and her French allies were besieged at the Leith, and when the Regent died shortly thereafter, an agreement was reached for both the French and English to withdraw from Scotland.

The Protestants were once again in the ascendancy. Laws favoring Protestantism were passed, the Roman church was disestablished, the mass was outlawed, and Scotland was declared by Parliament to be Protestant. Of course, the Roman Catholic church remained, and many people still considered themselves to be Catholic. Human nature being what it is, I'm afraid that we Protestants now became as intolerant of Catholics, as they had been of us.

We still had to organize a Scottish Reformed church. We created a General Assembly, composed of lay people and clergy, to govern the new church. We adopted a Confession of Faith, a Book of Discipline, and a Book of Worship. Many liturgical elements such as holy water, incense, sacraments other than baptism and the Lord's Supper, and confession to a priest were removed. Three orders of administration were set up: Ministers, Elders, and Deacons. Churches were to be under the governance of elders. The word we were using for "elders" was the Greek word *presbuteroi*, so the church eventually became known as the Presbyterian church.

It was my hope that Scotland would now be left free of foreign alliances and that the Reformed church could grow to be the Church of Christ in Scotland. It was not to be so simple. In 1560 Francis, the King of France, died. Mary Stuart was now free to return to Scotland to take over her own throne. She also saw it as her mission to restore the Roman Catholic church in Scotland.

Over the next few years I had numerous visits with the young queen. We were always civil toward one another, and I acknowledged her sovereignty, in spite of the impediment of her sex. I protested my loyalty to her, but she said she felt that in a showdown the people would follow me and not her. She said privately to others that she thought I was the most dangerous man in Scotland. She had a keen mind and a sharp tongue, and neither of us felt that we could soften our views. Eventually Mary got into domestic trouble, and was forced to abdicate in favor of her son.

Parliament was called, the Reformed church was designated as the established church, and it was decreed thereafter all kings, at the time of their coronation, shall take an oath to maintain the established religion. The continuance of the Reformed Church of Scotland was now as assured as it could be. It was time for me to return to my pulpit at Saint Giles in Edinburgh.

My reason for telling you all this is to remind you that any freedom of religion you now have was purchased at great cost by those who have gone before you. Be courageous in standing for the right as God gives you the ability to see the right. It is appropriate to resist the laws of the state when those laws are unjust. Let us never give absolute sovereignty to those who have authority over us, even when it is dangerous for us to resist. The only absolute sovereign is God. Under that sovereignty, all of us regardless of position, stand as servants.

It is important to be vigilant, for as all people are sinners, all will attempt to enforce their opinions if there are not checks and balances. Where I myself have been intolerant, I pray for God's mercy, and I ask you who would judge me to remember the circumstances under which I was laboring. May God bless the church of Jesus Christ everywhere.

ALL SAINTS SUNDAY

As Thousands Cheer
Hebrews 11:32—12:1

When basketball player Scott Wedman was traded from the Kansas City Kings to the Boston Celtics he was delighted. Not that he had anything against his former team, he was just elated to be part of the most successful team in professional basketball history. When he first donned a Celtic uniform and looked up at all those championship banners suspended from the rafters in Boston Garden, he said it had an uplifting effect on him.

"It was as if the 'ghosts' of past Celtic starts were up there cheering on the current players," he said. Present-day New York Yankee baseball players testify to the same emotion when they play in Yankee Stadium, with the center field plaques behind them honoring such immortals as Babe Ruth, Lou Gehrig, Joe DiMaggio, and Mickey Mantle. As one player put it: "The 'legends' urge you to play your best — it's as if they're watching how you're doing."

What one termed "ghosts" in Boston Garden and "legends" in Yankee Stadium are called a "cloud of witnesses" in the Bible. The writer of the book of Hebrews mentions a list of "stars" or "heroes" of our religious tradition. He then goes on to suggest that we and they are bound together in an endless relay race in which each of us receives the baton from those who have gone before, we carry it for a while, and we pass it on to those who come after us. As each of us passes on the baton we, in our turn, take our places in the stands and continue to cheer on those who are still running. As we gather on this All Saints Sunday, we have remembered those in our congregation who have died during the past year. These and others have become a part of a great host of interested but unseen spectators who, by the thousands, are cheering us on and applauding our victories. What they have passed on to us is the conviction that God is a God of love who touches our lives through experiences of love that we are to pass on. For me, this has been a week of remembering — calling to mind those persons, now largely departed, who have contributed to my understanding that I am loved, I am a person of worth.

The first thing I would like to do this morning is to share with you some of the instances through which God's love has become clearer to me. This part of the journey will be largely personal, and I beg your indulgence for that. It is my hope that, as I mention individuals who have conveyed God's love to me, your own memory and imagination will take over and put other names to similar experiences so that, with me, you will give thanks for the way God has touched you through others.

Most of us, I suppose, would start with our families, for there most of us have experienced nurturing love. I think of my mother as one who sought ways to make me aware that I must take responsibility for the consequences of my actions. The third time I set fire to the wood bin in the basement of the house by playing with matches, she took me to the fire station where those big, burly men told me that children who play with matches go to jail. On another occasion, when a young friend and I, seeking to impress some girls, stole cosmetics from the drugstore and got found out, she took me to the police station where I sat on a bench, a quivering lump of humanity, while she went into the sergeant's office, she said to plead with them not to put me into prison this time. For years, whenever I came to a firehouse or a police station, I crossed the street lest they identify me and take me in. I also stopped playing with matches and stealing. Her action helped me to see subsequently that love does not indulge us. It tries to correct our weaknesses in order to bring out the good.

I remember my dad for pancake evangelism. Sunday morning was Mom's day not to have to make breakfast. On the other hand, they wanted us to get up for Sunday school. So every Sunday morning, Dad got up early and made pancakes, not only for us, but for any kids in the neighborhood who would accompany us to Sunday school. It wasn't uncommon for me to have four friends to Sunday breakfast. There were other parents sleeping in and we were offering the best deal in the neighborhood, even if it did include having to go to Sunday school. What it said to me, and to the other kids was that somebody thought it was important enough to put himself out so that we would get religious instruction.

Another group from whom I received the message of love was the church — in fact, over the years, from a number of churches. When I was a little tyke attending the Norwegian Methodist Church with my family, there was an older gentleman by the name of Mr. Warenskjold, who used to give wrapped candy to the children. It made going to church a little sweeter than it might have been. The candy meant someone cared for us.

In another church there was a preacher who was pretty negative about most other groups, pretty narrow about beliefs, but he took an interest in my eternal soul, and it was under his ministry with all its weaknesses that I really heard the gospel and became a follower of Christ.

There was a high school Sunday school teacher, Phil Philibosian, who helped me to feel that it was possible to take the faith seriously and still be a thinking person.

When I was going to college near the tiny community of Big Pine and thought that maybe God was calling me to the ministry, Carrie Oval, an elderly woman pastor of the church in that community, without even knowing me, allowed me to preach my first sermon to her unsuspecting flock. She trusted me.

Bob Wallace, a Methodist preacher from Maryland, whom I met while we were both attending Army Chaplains' School, graciously invited me to preach in his church, though I was a Baptist. He so impressed me with the openness of the Methodist church that he changed the course of my ministry.

Bishop Gerald Kennedy took a chance and gave me the opportunity to come into the Methodist church, though he knew little about me. He made me feel that I had something to offer. He also taught me how to preach.

Christian writers and preachers such as Harry Emerson Fosdick and Leslie Weatherhead have taught me that it is okay to doubt and to have reservations about some aspects of the faith. They have reminded me through their books that we are loved by God, not because we believe, but because we are loved. I learned from them that I did not have to earn God's love.

There are those in school who provided encouragement. I still remember with fondness my sixth grade teacher, Miss Magnison, who took an interest in me, encouraged me to write and to speak, and felt that there was something inside me that needed expression. Fourteen years after I left the sixth grade, I wrote to her to tell her I had become a minister. She was part of whatever came of it, for she gave encouragement.

Of course, there have been friends who have shaped the meaning of love. Doug and Caroline Charles, Presbyterian missionaries to Brazil, invited me to spend two weeks with them at their mission station in the interior of Brazil while I was still in high school. I observed how love is shaped into service; how it gives up home and family and country and comfort in order to minister to others. Ambrose Whytal, crippled by polio while still a young man, never to walk upright again and never free of pain, continued to coach a boys' basketball team and to be animated about a game he could no longer play. He was determined to have something to give, no matter how difficult. His coaching was love.

There was Gloie Boblitt, stricken with inoperable cancer, talking with me calmly and repeatedly about her coming death. She prepared a funeral service that was an uplifting celebration of life. She strengthened the faith of her friends and passed on to all an assurance that death does not have to defeat us. Her confidence inspired faith that God loves us in spite of the death of the body. Bill Coombs was afflicted with polio as a young adult and was paralyzed from the neck down. He was confined for years to a rocking bed, which forced his lungs to expand so that he could breathe. Family and friends frequently gathered at his home, in his room, to share potluck suppers in his presence. A sign over his bed reflected his own spirit. It said, "Halitosis is better than no breath at all." From him I learned to prize life as a gift and to see that it is possible to live life victoriously in the face of great difficulty.

There are many others still living, who continue to have a profound influence on me, but on this All Saints Sunday it seemed especially appropriate to remember those who have finished the course and have themselves entered the cheering section. From these people I have learned important lessons about God's love for me and for others. They have given me the baton. It is important that I pass it on.

But how do we pass on the baton? I think we do it by little acts of love. Whenever we do something that tells someone they are worthwhile, whenever we show an act of kindness, whenever we help someone to stand up straight, to have a little dignity, we are helping to create a world in which the God of love becomes more visible.

We expect this to happen in families. It doesn't always, but that is certainly the first place we look for it. Several years ago I served on the Conference Board of the Ordained Ministry. It is that board's responsibility to interview and examine candidates for ministry. It is an awesome responsibility for the board, but you can imagine the kind of anxiety it raises in the candidates. I remember one candidate who was relaxed, smiling, and confident. He was a joy to interview. In the course of the interview someone asked him if his wife was supportive of his entrance into the ministry. He smiled and pulled out an envelope. He said he had arrived for the interview nervous and apprehensive. Going through his pockets he had found a note his wife had written and placed in his pocket that morning. In the note she assured him of her love and that whatever the outcome they would face it together. Her assurance had given him confidence. We were delighted to get such a team. Love is expressed in little things.

John Drescher, in his book *If I Were Starting My Family Again*, tells of another revelation of love in little things. "When I was around thirteen and my brother was ten," he writes, "father promised to take us to the circus. But at lunchtime there was a phone call, some urgent business required his attention downtown. My brother and I braced ourselves for the disappointment. Then we heard him say, 'No, I won't be down. It will have to wait.' When he came back to the table, Mother smiled and said, 'The circus keeps coming back, you know.' 'Yes, I know,' said Father, 'but childhood doesn't.' " There were two lucky sons who knew they were important.

Sometimes that love is experienced in more painful circumstances. Moss Hart, the playwright, tells of an experience he shared with his father just before Christmas when Hart was ten years old. "Tugging at my father's coat I started down the line of pushcarts... I would merely pause before a pushcart to say, with as much control as I could muster, 'Look at that chemistry set!' or, 'There's a stamp album!' or, 'Look at that printing press!' Each time my father would pause and ask the pushcart man the price. Then, without a word, we would move on to the next pushcart. Once in a while he would pick up a toy of some kind and look at it and then at me, as if to suggest that this might be something I might like, but I was ten years old and a good deal beyond just a toy; my heart was set on a chemistry set or a printing press. There they were on every pushcart we stopped at, but the price was always the same, and soon I looked up and saw that we were nearing the end of the line of pushcarts. My father looked up, and I heard him jingle some coins in his pocket. In a flash I knew it all. He'd gotten together about 75 cents to buy me a Christmas present, and he hadn't dared to say so in case there was nothing to be had for so small a sum. As I looked up at him I saw a look of despair and disappointment in his eyes that brought me closer to him than I had ever been in my life. I wanted to throw my arms around him and say, 'It doesn't matter... I understand... This is better than a chemistry set or a printing press... I love you.'" Hart did not get a chemistry set or a printing press that Christmas, but he knew that he was loved, and it enabled him to love in return.

 The church too is a place where the baton is passed on to us. Chris Arp was a baker from Germany who was devoted to his church, but he was not particularly gifted as a speaker. One Christmas he baked gingerbread houses for every child in the Sunday school. The next year he did the same. For fifty years it was a tradition for children to receive one of his lovely creations. Children's children and grandchildren received his handiwork. As far as they were concerned, "Nothin' spells lovin' like somethin' from the oven," and Chris Arp said it best.

 In another congregation I served, Dr. Milo Brooks taught Sunday school for longer than anybody could remember. I heard stories of how he enlivened the lesson with baby opossums and little animals. He used his woodworking skills to create teaching aids. There are adults in that congregation who were taught by Milo when they were children. That is passing on the baton of faith! And the love is remembered long after the lesson is forgotten.

Sometimes love is passed on in business and in casual relationships. Harry Stein, a magazine editor, tells how he experienced it a few years back. "At dusk on the Friday of Labor Day weekend, 1973, ten miles short of Indianapolis, the old Chevy, in which we had driven from the East Coast to the West and nearly back again, finally gave out. Weary and almost out of money, we limped into a gas station off the highway. The owner-mechanic's diagnosis came in five minutes: our drive shaft was shot; we needed a new one. My face fell. 'How much will it cost?' I asked. He studied us — disheveled 24 year olds, and our useless vehicle for a moment. 'Wait here,' he said. And then, to his assistant, 'Eddie, I'll be back in a while.' Though the place was to have closed in an hour for the weekend, the owner was gone until after 10:00 pm. When he returned he brought with him a used drive shaft, found after searching every auto junkyard in town." "How much do we owe you?" asked Stein, quickly adding, "we only have $35; we'll send you the rest." The owner furrowed his brow. "Well, let's see," he said. "It'll cost you fifteen bucks for gas to get to New York, and you'll need a motel room tonight, and you've gotta eat... let's say seven dollars." "Seven dollars? That's ridiculous," said Stein. "Nope, seven dollars it is." "Then," says Stein, "after I'd stopped resisting and paid him his money, he clapped a hand on my shoulder and smiled a smile I'll remember for years. 'Have a good weekend,' he said." Stein may not have called it love, but that is what he was receiving, and he would remember it for the rest of his life. Receiving and passing on love in countless little ways that scarcely seem to be love at the moment — that is what the race is all about.

At the outset of my message, I mentioned Paul's suggestion that we are all involved in a race. One race that is extremely demanding is the triathlon, which involves a person swimming two miles, bicycling a hundred miles, and running 26 miles. I have a friend who recently participated in a triathlon event in Hawaii which is different from the individual triathlon. In this event, participants entered as teams. One fellow did the swimming, a second did the bicycling, a third did the running. The first one could do his part excellently and go to the stands. The second one could do likewise. But there was no victory for the team until the third one did his part to complete the work of the other two. You can imagine that there was great shouting and encouragement by each team member for the one still competing, but there was no completion until each one had contributed his part. Some parts took great time and energy. Others took less time and energy, but all were equally important to the completion.

In the race in which we are involved, we are being cheered on by those who have gone before. Some of them may have been great saints; others hardly saints at all. But the task will not be completed without the contribution of every one of us. And the task is to create a loving world. Every day the cloud of witnesses, numbering into the thousands, is cheering us on. Let's be sure we give it our best.

CHRIST THE KING SUNDAY

A Higher Loyalty
Matthew 13:31-33, 44-52

My parents were immigrants from Norway. For some reason my mother did not apply for citizenship for many years. When she did do so, I was a child of about eight. She went to citizenship classes and told me that she would have to be able to answer certain questions put to her by a judge. I was greatly distressed. "If you couldn't answer the questions," I asked, "would they put you on a boat and send you back to Norway?" She assured me that that wouldn't happen. My fears were unnecessary. She passed the examination and became a citizen. I asked her what she had to say as she became an American citizen. She said that she had to openly declare her loyalty to the United States of America, and if need be, to rise to its defense. Some of your parents may have had to do the same. Perhaps some of you were presented with that choice.

Most of us, however, don't get the chance to choose our loyalties — at least not our national ones — they are the result of the accident of birth. As a consequence, our loyalties may be unexamined.

Throughout his ministry, Jesus challenged his hearers to examine their loyalties, and if they found that what they were loyal to was unsatisfying, he invited them to commit themselves to a higher loyalty — one that he called the kingdom of God. Matthew, who recorded the words we read this morning, did not feel comfortable using the name of God, so he says Jesus was calling people to consider the kingdom of heaven, which means the same thing. Unfortunately, while Jesus often described what that kingdom is like, he never defined it. From what he did say, however, we can make out that Jesus was not so much talking about a place as about a relationship. It is that relationship in which we accept God's sovereignty over our lives. We enter the kingdom when we decide to dethrone all lesser considerations, including self, and to pledge our allegiance to the reign of God in our own lives. Since we are called to become citizens of that kingdom, we ought to become as informed as we can about what that kingdom is like.

In the first parable read this morning Jesus said, "The kingdom of heaven is like a mustard seed that someone took and sowed in his field; it is the smallest of all seeds, but when it has grown it is the greatest of shrubs." I think what Jesus is suggesting here is that whatever God's kingdom may be one day, it starts out as the smallest of things. Ideas which have changed civilization have often begun with one person. The great advances of the race have often started without any trumpets sounding or anybody being aware that anything exceptional was taking place.

On the 100th anniversary of Abraham Lincoln's birth, John McCutcheon drew a famous cartoon. He showed two Kentucky backwoodsmen standing at the edge of a wood in the winter. One asks the other, "Anything new?" The other man replies, "Nothing much. Oh, there's a new baby over at Tom Lincoln's. But you know, nothing significant ever happens around here."

Centuries before that, someone might have asked in Bethlehem, "Anything new?" And the answer might have been, "No, nothing new. Oh, they say a woman named Mary had a baby in a stable last night. But nothing significant ever happens around here." George MacDonald wrote of that birth:

They all were looking for a king
To slay their foes and lift them high:
Thou cam'st, a little baby thing
That made a woman cry.
(George MacDonald, 1919, "That Holy Thing")

And when that child grew up and taught, it was of little things: a cup of cold water, a person with one talent, a widow's offering, a lost coin, kindness done for "one of the least of these." And subsequently, how insignificant the movement must have appeared: a teacher on a hillside, a man slain on a cross, a borrowed grave, twelve unlearned followers, and one of them was a traitor. So many of God's greatest happenings begin so unobtrusively that they appear at the moment no more important than the planting of a mustard seed. But therein lies our hope, for the seed God plants in every one of us, may, in God's good time, put forth its branches for the benefit of all. God's reign may start off as something small in us, but it has the potential to grow as others pledge their allegiance to it and come under its sway.

In a second parable Jesus said, "The kingdom of heaven is like yeast that a woman took and put into three measures of flour until all was leavened." As a child I used to help with the baking of bread in our home. I remember breaking up the cakes of yeast, dissolving them in the liquid ingredients, mixing that with the flour, and then letting the dough sit for a while so that the yeast could do its work. It worked silently, invisibly, transforming the dough from something flat to something light and palatable. During that rising process the dough had to be pummeled once or twice, pushing it back down to get rid of air bubbles so that the texture would be more consistent. It took time to accomplish and sometimes there was nothing to do but wait.

What Jesus seems to be saying here is that it is the work of the kingdom to influence the world, not to turn the world into the kingdom. The kingdom cannot always be seen, because it is working within the lives of individuals and through them influencing the world. Christianity has often been too optimistic about what the church can accomplish. Many have assumed that it was our responsibility to bring in God's kingdom — to make the world into a utopia of peace and prosperity. That is indeed our vision, but not necessarily our responsibility. If we are supposed to be turning this world into the kingdom of God, there is an awful lot going on to discourage us: the Holocaust of World War II, ethnic cleansing in Bosnia, savage tribal strife in Rwanda and Burundi, terrorist attacks all over the world, racial hatred in our own country. For every step forward, there is a step backward.

What I want to suggest is that God has not given us exclusive responsibility for all that is to be done. In the first parable, Jesus does not use the illustration of an acorn becoming a giant oak tree or a seed becoming one of the great cedars of Lebanon with which his audience would have been acquainted. Instead, it is a tiny seed that becomes a common shrub, just a step above a weed. In the second parable the dough is not turned into yeast — but the dough is influenced by the yeast, so that the dough is different from what it was. Our vision is a world without war, but perhaps all we can do is bind up the wounds of one victim; our vision is for a world without hunger, but perhaps all we can do is share canned goods through a food distribution center; our vision is a world free from ignorance, but perhaps all we can do is teach one person to read. In all those lesser activities God's kingdom is present, the mustard seed is planted, and the yeast is changing the situation of one person from hopelessness to hope.

Jesus went on to say that "the kingdom of heaven is like treasure hidden in a field, which someone found and hid; then in his joy he goes and sells all that he has and buys that field." Such situations were not unknown in Palestine. All through its history Israel was subject to invasions. There were no dependable banks or safe deposit boxes. As the enemy descended upon the land, a person would often bury coins in the ground, intending to come back and dig them up when the danger was past. But the burier could be killed or carted off to die in exile, and his cache go undiscovered.

Generations later a poor tenant farmer might accidentally unearth the treasure and learn how important it could be to own that field. We can envision that person looking every which way to see whether he had been noticed, covering his find, and running home to see what he could possibly do to purchase that field. The ethics of such a purchase is not in view here, only the joy of discovering something so special in the course of one's everyday routine.

What Jesus seems to be saying here is that the kingdom of God may be found in the mundane and ordinary as readily as in the spectacular. The famous scientist George Washington Carver called his busy laboratory, "God's Little Workshop." The name was indicative of the humility of this man who prayed for God's guidance in discovering the uses of what was then an unimportant crop: the peanut. He once shared that he had prayed the following prayer: "Dear Mr. Creator, tell me why the universe was made." "Ask something more in keeping with that little mind of yours," the Lord replied. "Dear Mr.

Creator, what was mankind made for?" Again the Lord said, "You ask too much. Cut down the extent of your request and improve the intent." So Carver tried again. "Mr. Creator, will you tell me why the peanut was made?" "That's better," the Lord said and from that day Mr. Carver developed over 300 uses for the peanut. He found treasure in something that was part of his everyday experience.

Finally, in this series of parables, Jesus said that "the kingdom of heaven is like a merchant in search of fine pearls; on finding one pearl of great value, he went and sold all that he had and bought it." I take this parable to mean that the kingdom of God is worth whatever it takes to possess it, because of the joy that comes from being part of it. Millard Fuller's father gave him a pig when he was a boy. As a result of that gift, while other boys in Lanett, Alabama, were concentrating on baseball or fishing, Millard became a livestock trader. He made enough money as a trader to put himself through college. While in law school, he sold holly wreaths, desk blotters, campus directories, and birthday cakes. He invested his profits in real estate. By graduation he was clearing $50,000 a year. He was looking for the good life and he felt that he knew how to find it.

By age 29, Millard Fuller was a millionaire with an estate-type home, a vacation retreat, two speedboats, a luxury automobile, and shares in three cattle ranches. One day Millard's wife left him, taking their two small children. "I don't feel I have a husband," she said. "You're always working and thinking about making money." In the aftermath of his wife's departure, Millard began to reflect on the meaning of his life. He had his first million at the age of 29; he had already set his next goal — to have ten million by the time he was 39. But when his wife, Linda, left him, he woke up to how much his "success" had cost him. He asked Linda for a chance to reconcile, which she granted. To get away from things for a while, they went to visit a project called "Koinonia Farms" near Americus, Georgia. They stayed there for a month, helping to replace dilapidated shacks and shanties of poor people. They had found a purpose.

The Fullers sold most of their possessions and founded a corporation to help poor people build houses for themselves and others. The Fullers then took their plan to Africa where they oversaw the building of 114 homes. They called their newfound mission "Habitat for Humanity." Included among their carpenters have been Jimmie and Rosalyn Carter. The Fullers' program has now placed houses for the poor in several hundred communities in this country and more than 25 nations around the world. Of their newfound purpose Millard says: "I don't believe we're saved by how many houses we put up. I don't believe that we're saved by how many poor people we feed. I know that we're saved by... Jesus and by the grace of God.... What matters is our response to what God has done. We believe that 'Habitat for Humanity' is one response, one manifestation of what God has done for us in Christ."

The kingdom of God starts out small, but its influence grows; we discover it in ordinary things, but eventually we come to know that it is worth more than anything else. When we decide to become followers of Jesus Christ, we become citizens of a new country. We become residents of the kingdom of God.

THANKSGIVING DAY

When the Good Times Roll
Deuteronomy 8:11-18

The people of Israel were about to enter the promised land. They had been through hardships for many years in the wilderness, but the nation had survived. The prospect was that their situation was soon going to change for the better. Moses, their leader, saw this as a good opportunity to bring certain things to their attention. He reminded them of their past hardships: slavery, terrors of wild beasts, thirst in the desert, and days when they were hungry. He further reminded them that when things had seemed the darkest, somehow the hand of God was always revealed. They had been delivered from slavery, rescued from wild beasts, given water where it was dry, and provided with food when they were at wit's end. In these crises they had been able to discern the hand of God. But Moses could foresee his people were headed into what could be even greater danger: the danger of losing contact with God because of self-satisfying prosperity. So Moses sought to offer his people a word of caution.

The first thing Moses did was to describe prosperity. If we were called upon to list some of the characteristics of the prosperous, what would they be? To dine at Spago's as often as we wished? To have a mansion along the coast? To drive a Rolls Royce? To do all of our shopping in Nieman Marcus? To have such extensive holdings that we need to be in constant contact with our stockbroker? Or better yet, to have our attorney in constant contact with our broker? For most of us, the prosperous person is someone else, someone much better off. We are just middle-class folks trying to get along.

But look at how Moses described prosperity. Prosperity has nothing to do with where one eats, but with whether one has enough to eat. "I can't forget their faces," writes Steve Reynolds, a worker with World Vision in Africa. "And I don't want to forget them. Their oversized eyes. The old man looks in the face of a four-year-old child. The despair in the face of a mother who has already lost her three children to starvation... These images I carry with me... Another child, Tanshane, one year old, has probably never had enough to eat. I wanted to tell Tanshane about other parts of the world where children laugh and play and eat candy until they get sick. But all I could do was watch him and hope that the supplementary food World Vision provided would be enough until his family could raise crops again." "Whoever has enough food," said Moses, "is prosperous."

Prosperity has nothing to do with where one's house is, said Moses, but with whether one has a place to live at all. Refugee camps in Africa are bursting with people fleeing tyranny and death, who cannot return to their homeland, and who are not welcome elsewhere. In Sudan, thousands of villagers who survived the destruction of their villages have fled to other villages that are in turn devastated. They have witnessed the brutal murder of close relatives and the total destruction of all that they value. When compared with those circumstances, whoever has a decent place to live is prosperous.

For many people, prosperity has little to do with whether one has need of a stockbroker or shops in Nieman Marcus, but much to do with whether basic needs are met. An article in *The New Republic* several years ago reminds us that no international frontier is more abrupt or brazen in matters of human condition than the border between the United States and Mexico. The quaintness and cruelty of this border is that it so starkly divides poor and rich. Across a hundred feet of the sluggish Rio Grande, infant mortality is twice the U.S. rate, life expectancy is ten years shorter, and the per capita income is barely a tenth of what the Americans enjoy. Geographically, Ciudad Juarez could be a suburb of El Paso, but financially they are worlds apart. For those on the south side of the border, prosperity would be to have been born a few hundred feet to the north.

Then prosperity is something that is relative to where one is. And relative to most of the world, we are the prosperous. Food may be scarce in some places, but most of us leave the table satisfied. For most of us, our housing is more than adequate. For most of us, the problem is not whether we have clothes to wear, but whether they are the right style or color. Some of us may not have much in the bank, but there are very few things of a material nature we cannot get — on credit if no other way — if we really desire them. I have a friend, a well-paid 747 pilot, who told me, "We don't have to keep up with the Joneses; we *are* the Joneses!" In the eyes of most of the world, we are the prosperous ones Moses was speaking about.

The second thing Moses did was to warn us that there are some real dangers related to prosperity. For one thing, it can produce pride. Rufus Jones once told a tale about the daughter of a prosperous egg rancher who came into a village store in Maine. Wanting to be friendly, the storekeeper smiled and started talking with her. "Are your hens laying now?" he asked. "They can," the girl replied with her nose in the air, "but in our financial position they don't have to." The ultimate in pride is to think that you can run an egg ranch without the help of the chickens.

Moses cautions that in prosperity people are tempted to take the credit for their own good fortune, saying, "My power and the might of my hand has gotten me this wealth." Prosperity can so blind us to the source of our wealth that we think we have made it all by ourselves. I read some interesting statistics recently. Whether they are true, I don't know, but the next time you sit down to a bowl of cereal, consider this. Our provident God puts into one acre of grain: 4 million pounds of water, 6800 pounds of oxygen, 5200 pounds of carbon, 162 pounds of nitrogen, 125 pounds of potassium, 75 pounds of sulphur, 50 pounds of magnesium, 50 pounds of calcium, 40 pounds of phosphorus, and 2 pounds of iron. That's 4 million, 12 thousand, 504 pounds of chemicals. That puts into a better perspective how much *we* contribute to what we eat. Pride can blind us to the part that God plays.

Prosperity can also produce hardness of heart. When we have nothing, we are quite prepared to share it; when we have something, we become protective and fearful that we will lose it. I love to hear those words of Emma Lazarus carved on our Statue of Liberty: "Give me your tired, your poor, your huddled masses yearning to breathe free, the wretched refuse of your teeming shores; send these, the homeless, tempest-tossed to me. I lift my lamp beside the golden door." That is our heritage. We grew up believing it. But do we subscribe to it any longer? Does it apply to workers from Mexico? Is it true for refugees from Moslem counties? We have run out of frontier land. Now when we divide the pie the pieces get smaller for us and that makes us anxious. But woe to us if, in our abundance, we become so insulated from the misery of our brothers and sisters that we do not feel their pain and seek to relieve it.

Not only can prosperity cause us to shut our eyes to God and our hearts to God's children, it can cause us to lose sight of what is meaningful in our own lives. There is nothing wrong with being prosperous. One lady said, "I've been poor and unhappy, and I've been rich and unhappy. Believe me, being rich and unhappy is better." Some of us have been poor, and we have rightly fled the wretchedness of poverty, for being poor, of itself, has little to commend it. Most of us have probably had to work pretty hard for what we have, but the problem is that the pursuit of prosperity tends to become all-consuming because we feel that we always need a little more and that causes us to forget why we are here.

I was talking with a friend of mine who is a theoretical physicist working for a large corporation. He is supposed to spend his time thinking and coming up with new ideas. I asked him if he owned stock in the company. He said he did not own any stock, for he felt that concern about such things had ruined many fine scholars. In fact, he said, if you had a colleague in your field who was vying with you for a promotion, it would be in your interest to give him a hundred shares of some successful stock. Pretty soon he would be reading the *Wall Street Journal* instead of scholarly journals, and you would get the promotion. I'm afraid that a number of us are like that. If we enjoy a little prosperity, we want more, and our eyes are taken off of the more important goal of becoming all that we can be as children of God. When we are doing well, we have to be very careful.

The third thing Moses did was to offer a way to deal with the dangers of prosperity. He said when these good things come your way, "Remember the Lord your God." What does that mean? For one thing, I think that means acknowledging God as the source of our blessings. In his inspirational book *To Kiss the Joy*, Robert

Raines tells of a double surprise he got in rounding a bend on a mountain road on a trip through the West. The first surprise was the glorious scene he discovered as he came around a curve: a deep blue lake with ranges of pyramid pines stretching for miles beyond. He was taken aback with the beauty of it. The second surprise was that as he pulled off the road to enjoy the scene, another fellow drove up, gazed for a while, then got a trumpet out of the trunk of his car and began to blow a heart-felt song of appreciation for what he was seeing. He was, he said, returning thanks to God.

What we give thanks for will vary according to our ability to appreciate. Whatever we are thankful for, the important thing is acknowledgment of the source.

To remember the Lord also means to acknowledge responsibility for what we have received. In Europe there are cathedrals that took as long as 600 years to complete. Those who started them made great plans, but the projects were brought to completion only as subsequent generations took responsibility for what was handed to them, made improvements, and passed on what had come to them. What each generation received was to be enjoyed, but it was also held in trust for others.

A few years ago, just before Thanksgiving, Mario Cuomo, then governor of New York, heard about a mother of ten in Schenectady who was having a tough time trying to buy the essentials of a Thanksgiving meal on her school-bus driver's salary. The governor had just received a check for $1,000 as an honorarium for speaking to a Writers' Club. He donated the check to an organization called Concern for the Hungry. One of the recipients was the bus driver who, years before, had helped to establish the fund for the assistance of needy families. Cuomo's contribution went into the fund, whose workers expected to feed 2,000 families that Thanksgiving.

Can we do anything like that? Yes, we can. This church operates a food distribution center for the benefit of the needy. One can give food, scrip, or funds here any Sunday. To act responsibly toward what we have received involves asking ourselves, "What am I to do with the good things that have been entrusted to me?"

Finally remembering the Lord means expressing gratitude. The golf pro, Gary Player, was born into poverty in South Africa. He recalls his childhood as one of loneliness, pain, and poverty. His mother died when he was eight, and his father worked long hours in the mines. "We were so poor," he says, "that I used to take off my shoes whenever I could so they'd last longer." After years of practice, Player turned professional in 1953. He won more than 150 tournaments and earned large amounts of prize money in addition to the $1 million a year he made from product endorsements. Though he is clearly successful, Player is careful never to forget the real source of his success: "Golf is the talent God loaned me," he says. "You have no idea how often I get down on my knees in gratitude."

Have we acquired wealth? It is an important corrective to see that God provided the energy. Have we studied hard and gotten a good education? It is God who gave the brain. Have we become successful in our business? It is God who provided the opportunities. I am not suggesting that our own determination, hard work, and risk-taking don't count. I am only suggesting that we humbly acknowledge that we have received more than we have given and that gratitude, therefore, is in order.

When we are confronted with adversity, it is not difficult for most of us to cry out to God. But when the good times roll, it is easy for us to say, "My power and my might have gotten me where I am." It is then that we need to remember the Lord — to acknowledge God's place in our life, to exercise responsibility for what has been put into our hands, and to express gratitude for what we have received.

CHRISTMAS EVE

Are You Ready for Christmas?
Titus 2:11-15

On July 14, 1789, Jean Lenoir a cobbler living in an obscure street of Paris wrote in his diary: "Nothing of importance happened today." Just a short distance away was the Bastille. On that very day a mob had stormed it, killed troops, freed prisoners, destroyed the building, and started the French Revolution. That event changed the whole life of France, but Jean Lenoir missed it.

Too often, I am afraid, this is the way it is with us at Christmas. Christmas comes and we are busy with the details of preparing for a holiday. The festivities are nice, but they pass into New Year's Day without our ever getting around to considering the revolutionary impact Christmas has had on the world. We sing over and over again of the babe born in Bethlehem, but do we ask ourselves why he was born, or why we sing? It is possible to go through a great event such as Christmas commemorates, and feel with Jean Lenoir that "nothing important has happened." And truly, unless something has happened *in us*, it is correct to say "nothing has happened," as far as we are concerned.

What ought to happen if Christmas is to have any personal significance for us is that we should begin a style of life that the church from the very beginning has called salvation. It is the possibility of that "style of life" which makes Christmas a significant day at all. It is that "style of life" which the apostle Paul was talking about when, in his own theological language, he spoke of the Advent of Christ, for in his mind Christmas and salvation were tied together.

The first thing Paul points out is that salvation has a past dimension. In the New English Bible, Paul is translated as saying, "The grace of God has dawned upon the world." I like that word "dawned," for I see in it the image of darkness being challenged. Some years ago I had an experience that helped me to appreciate what darkness means. My wife and I had arrived in Cortina d' Ampezzo in Italy in the off season and found most of the hotels closed. The one that was open had what appeared to be a nice room that fronted on a highway going up a hill. When we went to bed we discovered that every truck in Italy was trying to make it up that hill, shifting through all sixteen gears as they went. First, I closed all the windows, then all the drapes, with only a modest effect. The room did have a wooden storm shutter that could be lowered by means of a belt. I lowered the shutter and suddenly we were cut off from the world. No sound, no light, no air. With the lights on I easily returned to bed, put out the light, and went to sleep.

When I awoke I could see nothing. I couldn't find the clock, much less see its dial. I couldn't remember what the room looked like or where the furniture was positioned. I called to Mary to see if she felt that it was time to get up. She thought so but was not about to leave the safety of the bed. I groped about, seeking something familiar, but everything seemed unfamiliar or downright hostile. I stepped in an open suitcase, scraped my shin, there was stumbling, cursing (from where I can't imagine), and then down on all fours crawling to the wall to see if I could find the strap to lift the shutter. When I finally found the strap and lifted the shutter, light came pouring in and we could get our bearings and see clearly to avoid those things that had seemed so hostile. There was plenty of light outside, but we had been groping in the dark.

I don't wish to overstate the case, but in some respects that experience parallels our human situation. In a world darkened by greed, hatred, selfishness, guilt, and ignorance, we stumble, lose our way, get lost, hurt ourselves, and hurt others. We experience the world as hostile, we become fearful, anxious, lonely, sensing that we are cut off from others. We are in the dark. But upon this darkness, Paul says, the light has dawned.

There is a tombstone on an island in the South Pacific marking the grave of the first missionary who came to that island. On the tombstone it says, "Before he came there was no light; when he left, there was no darkness." This is how Paul saw the coming of Jesus Christ. Light has come to challenge the darkness, and the darkness can no longer keep us prisoner.

In the New Testament, Jesus' coming is referred to as the entrance of light. "In him was life, and the life was the light of humanity" (John 1:4). "The true light that enlightens everyone was coming into the world" (John 1:9). And John had Jesus say, "I am the light of the world" (John 8:12).

To return to Paul, he said that the grace of God has dawned. I read somewhere that we are receiving light from stars two billion light years away. In other words, the light that filters down to our telescopes from these galaxies started its journey before any life at all appeared on our earth, at a time when our earth was still a smoldering lump of molten rock and lava.

God's grace, revealed in Jesus, also has a past dimension. A definite person, Jesus, was born in a definite place, Bethlehem, at a definite time in the past, when Herod was king in Jerusalem. That coming was so inconspicuous that had Jean Lenoir been living in that area, he would no doubt have written, "Nothing of importance happened today." But something *was* happening: God was getting ready. A beacon was being prepared; a light to guide those who are in the dark; a light to warn of dangers; a light to attract the lost.

A number of years ago I accompanied some friends on an overnight cruise to Catalina on a small boat. We stayed longer the next day than we should have, so that on our return trip darkness fell, the clouds rolled in, the wind came up and began to stir the waves so that we felt like we were on a roller coaster. The compass began to act up, so we were no longer sure of our course. We felt lost, with nothing to guide us. After more than an hour of tension, we spotted a light, and it gave us something toward which to steer. We were not sure what it was, but it represented salvation from aimless wandering. It turned out to be the beacon at San Pedro harbor, and it guided us to safety. Our safe return was brought about by a light that someone had erected long ago.

I want to suggest Christmas is like that. God was preparing for our salvation a long time ago. In the person of Christ, God was reaching down into our world and offering hope. He was providing a light to guide us to safety, so we would not have to be tossed every which way with no hope of being saved. That dimension of our salvation was accomplished in the past.

But Paul went on to suggest that our salvation has a present dimension. The process of salvation was initiated by God. In the coming of Christ, to which we look back every Christmas, God has attempted to capture our attention. A guiding light has been provided. Christ calls us to a way of life which, he says, will bring us to fulfillment, but we still have to make the choice as to whether we will follow it and make it a part of our present circumstances.

Paul suggested several ways in which our salvation is experienced in the present. One of those is the exercise of self-control. Paul called it temperance. Unfortunately, because of the influence of the rather narrow Puritans who helped start this country, temperance has come to mean abstinence from practically everything. There are those who feel that if anything is fun, it must be sinful; good times are frowned upon. Instead of the fullness of life Jesus offered, such people make the Christian life a rather dull gray.

I much prefer the attitude of Sister Damien Flood, a nun and professor of theology at Springfield College in Illinois, who said: "If I had my life to live over, I'd try to make more mistakes. I would relax. I would limber up. I would be sillier than I have been this trip. I know of very few things I would take seriously. I would be crazier. I would be less hygienic. I would take more chances. I would take more trips. I would climb more mountains, swim more rivers, watch more sunsets. I would burn more gasoline, eat more ice cream. I'd have more real problems and fewer imaginary ones... I have been one of those people who do not go anywhere without a thermometer, a hot water bottle, a raincoat, and a parachute. If I had it to do over again, I would go places and do things and travel lighter. I'd ride more merry-go-rounds and pick more daisies." I think that spirit is in accord with the spirit of Jesus, who was criticized by the pious people of his day because he spent time among those who were celebrating and having a good time. The Christian life does not have to be dull gray.

This does not mean that we don't have to take Paul's call for self-control seriously. The Greek philosopher, Plato, compared the life of each of us to a carriage drawn by a pair of spirited horses.

In the carriage the driver holds the reins and guides the horses on a straight and smooth road. But one day a heavy drowsiness comes upon the driver and he falls asleep at the reins. The horses, not feeling the restraint of the reins, go off the right path, and soon they are speeding over hill and valley. In their mad flight they come nearer and nearer to the edge of a deep gorge. At that moment a man standing nearby and seeing the threatened danger, calls out to the driver in a loud voice: "Wake up! Save yourself!" With a start, the driver suddenly awakens. In a moment he realizes his peril. Hastily he grasps the reins and exerting almost superhuman effort, he succeeds in swerving the horses away from the gorge, thereby saving his own life and those of his animals. These fiery steeds are the desires and the passions to which the hearts of people incline from their youth. The driver is the will God has given people so that they might rule over their desires and have dominion over their impulses.

As Christians we need to affirm our appetites as God-given capacities, but we also need to be in control of them and not have them in control of us. Some things are destructive for us, and we need to know what to avoid. A temperate lifestyle allows us to acknowledge the power of temptation, while at the same time appreciating the goodness of God's world. It is part of our salvation.

A second way, Paul said, that we demonstrate salvation in the present is through honesty. I read an article on dishonesty recently which indicated that hotels and motels lose $1.5 billion a year in stolen towels, bedding, and fixtures. It is estimated that one in every three guests leaves with something not his own. Doctors, the article says, take stethoscopes from hospitals, and nurses take home linens to the tune of $1,000 per bed annually — money that must be recovered from patient charges. Two Washington clergymen were found to be pocketing thousands of dollars from food stamps sold through their church.

Paul calls us to a higher standard than that. Tom Watson has been called one of the greatest golfers in the world. He has won nearly every major golf tournament at least once, and many of them several times. Fame and fortune have not spoiled him. He is respected as well as admired by those who have followed his outstanding career.

Both his skill and integrity were evident at an early age. He had his heart set on becoming a champion. He also had his personal code of honor firmly in mind. In the first state tournament that he ever entered, he put his putter down behind his ball on one of the greens. To his dismay, the ball moved slightly. No one saw it but him; of that he was certain. He was under great pressure to win, and there was not time to add up the pluses and minuses of the alternatives. But he knew without hesitation what he must do; he went over to an official and said, "My ball moved." That action cost him a stroke, but Tom Watson placed his personal integrity ahead of his keen desire to win. That is the kind of standard Christians are called to emulate: being honest, even though it may be costly.

A third way in which we demonstrate our salvation in the present is by our openness toward God. Paul calls this a life of godliness. The situation of many people is not that they are atheists who deny God or that they are wicked people who are just waiting to do something evil, but their lives have no spiritual dimension. As a result, they are not tuned in to life's full potential. Years ago, when I was just setting up housekeeping, someone gave me a used monaural record player. It wasn't the best, but it played music. Not knowing about such things, I went out and bought a stereophonic record. It sounded terrible. The potential for great music was on the record, but I wasn't able to tap that potential with my monaural player. The life each of us is given is stereophonic. We have a physical nature and a spiritual nature. If all we are experiencing is the physical side, then we are depriving ourselves of a whole dimension of life and living our lives monaurally. God, we are told, is a spirit. When we exercise the spiritual side of our nature, we are opening ourselves to God and experiencing salvation in the present.

The final dimension of salvation Paul mentions is the future. Again, in the New English Bible, he said, "Looking forward to the happy fulfillment of our hopes, when the splendor of God appears." There is something about our salvation that is always future. If we were lost at sea in the black of night, a beacon on the shore could be the beginning of our salvation from hopelessness and lostness. If we set our course toward that light, we would be in the process of being saved. But it is not until we come into the safe harbor, toward which the beacon is guiding us, that our salvation is complete.

While we wait for our salvation to be complete, it is the light that God sent that gives us hope. A young writer had just finished his first short story. He felt that he had produced a masterpiece. Anxiously, he read it to a wise old author. It was a story about the son of a poor widow who lived in a humble cottage in the Peru Valley of upstate New York. One day the boy set out for the big city to earn his fortune. Before he left, his mother said to him: "Now remember, son, if you ever get into trouble, no matter how bad it is, you set off for home, and as you come over the hill, you'll always find a light burning in the window and I'll be waiting to welcome you." The story labored on — a lurid picture of the decline and fall of the hero, debauchery, crime, prison, and ultimate release. Then he decided to go home. Coming over the hill, he looked down on the outline of that little old cottage snuggled tightly in the evening gloom, and — there was no light burning. Immediately, the aged writer who was listening, vaulted off his chair and with vehemence yelled, "You young devil, put that light back!" As long as the light is visible, there is hope.

The light of which we have been speaking is the coming of Christ that we celebrate in this season. Christmas is God's own doing, and we do well to look back to it. But getting ready for Christmas is something that we do ourselves, by responding to God's action, and if we have not done that, then we are not really ready and Christmas will come and go without making any real difference in our lives. If we do respond by following the light that God has sent, then we are not only looking back on a great event that took place in the past, we are on course for that ultimate rendezvous: the spending of eternity with God.

There is in Melbourne, Australia, a building known as the Shrine of Remembrance. It was built to commemorate the people's sacrifices during World War I. It was so designed that at exactly 11:00 am on November 11 for 1,000 years, a beam of sunshine will shine through an opening in the dome and illumine the one word "Love" in the inscription reading "Greater love hath no man."

God, the great designer of the universe, has done something like that, for in the fullness of time he has caused the light of divine love to shine upon a child in a stable. Thereafter, through all the centuries of time, people have stood in humility and awe at the remembrance of that event, as we do today. But let us not be content with a remembrance of what God has done; let us see it as evidence of what God is doing now in our lives; let us receive it as a pledge of what God has in mind for the future that is unfolding before us every day.

CHRISTMAS DAY

The Child with Four Names
Isaiah 9:1-7

Long ago in Egypt a slave girl held in her arms a newborn infant for whom there seemed no hope. The oppressive taskmasters required that the child should die. The girl framed a floating cradle, put the boy in it, and pushed him out on the waters of the Nile to survive or to perish, she knew not which. The child survived and Moses grew to challenge the forces of oppression and led his people out of bondage.

Far more recently at the opening of the nineteenth century in our own country, a child was born in a rough cabin on Nolan's Creek in Kentucky. Nobody would have expected much to come from a child with such limited opportunities, but Abraham Lincoln went on to lead his people to abolish the practice of slavery.

Over and over again in the history of the race, when there has been some great job to do, God saw to it that a baby was born who could bring it to pass. Often, decisive births that can affect the course of history occur in an out-of-the-way place.

In the eighth century before Christ, a child was born who was to be king of his people. It was a perilous time. There were powerful and hostile neighbors. The inhabitants of his tiny country were filled with fear; the prospects for them were gloomy. When the young man acceded to the throne, the court prophet, Isaiah, wrote a coronation poem for the event. He suggested that the young monarch had just been born, for as a king was crowned it was assumed that he became a son of God. Without ever naming the king, Isaiah proclaimed that the king's reign would have an impact far and wide. So significant would be his reign that he would be called Wonderful Counselor, Mighty God, Everlasting Father, Prince of Peace. It is assumed that the one Isaiah had in mind was King Hezekiah of Judah. While Hezekiah was a good king, nothing about his reign merited the praise anticipated by the prophet, so people have looked elsewhere for the fulfillment of his words.

Some 700 years later, a baby was born of a lowly mother in an obscure village called Bethlehem on the far fringes of a powerful empire. It would have been madness to believe that such a child could ever have any impact on a world enamored of wealth and power and position. Yet we have gathered today, 2,000 years later, in the name of that child. As far as Christians are concerned, God did in that simple village what he had always been doing. He was raising up a child to do what needed to be done. There are many people who feel that those noble words of Isaiah uttered so many centuries before are more fulfilled by this child, born in a manger than by anyone else who has lived before or since. Let us think about what kind of a message Isaiah was trying to give as he described the coming of the child with four names.

The first name Isaiah uses reminds us of the need in each of us for inner peace. In our age of anxiety we have learned the need for counseling. Most of us are aware that there are tensions within us that threaten our stability and sometimes pull us apart. We sometimes ask ourselves, "Why did I do that?" and we don't know the answer. Alfred Adler, the psychotherapist, said that each of us is crippled at an early age by at least three cripplers: a feeling of inferiority, parental neglect, and parental pampering. These keep us from knowing who we are and from accepting ourselves. To understand ourselves, we sometimes need the help of a counselor. A sign in the office of a Los Angeles psychiatrist reads: "Specializing in people who have no idea who they are."

Isaiah says that God will provide someone who is a Wonderful Counselor, someone who will help us to figure out who we are. The 1982 film *Chariots of Fire* tells of the events that led to the refusal by Eric Liddell to run on Sunday in the 1924 Olympic Games and of his subsequent victory in the 400 meter race. In a biography of Liddell, Sally Magnusson tells how she was at first skeptical about Liddell. Everyone who knew Liddell had nothing but good to say of him. Surely, Magnusson thought, there must be feet of clay to be revealed somewhere. She did not find those defects, but instead, she found a man who worked at his faith, a man who gave his life as a missionary to China, a man who over and over was described by friends as Christlike. Through his devotion to Jesus Christ he had discovered who he was, what he ought to do, and the courage to do it. Jesus is that kind of a counselor, one who helps us to know who we are — children of God, erring children perhaps, but loved anyway.

The second name Isaiah used speaks of the desire of each of us to be associated with power. We tend to focus on military might as the way to exert our will in the world. The lesson of scripture is that God often works through different means.

In Isaiah's day too the focus was on military might, but he wanted to remind people that God was at work in other ways. Isaiah spoke of a child who would be called the mighty God, or perhaps more accurately, divine hero, someone chosen by God. But when God chooses a hero it isn't always for military reasons. The year 1809 was a discouraging one in European history. Napoleon was dominant. His battles and victories dominated the news. But there were things going on in 1809 that didn't make news at all. In that year Lincoln was born, and Gladstone, and Tennyson, and Edgar Allan Poe, and Oliver Wendell Holmes, and Mendelssohn, and Cyrus McCormick, the inventor of the harvester. At the very least, one must say that the world was not as hopeless as it looked. God was choosing God's heroes.

In the first century it looked as though Caesar had it all on his side. But a baby was born who set a new way of life in motion. The theologian, Oscar Cullman, has taken an image from World War II to describe God's work in Christ. He likens the advent of Jesus to D-Day. The decisive battle with evil was won in his life, death, and resurrection. V-Day has not yet come. Therefore, we live between D-Day and V-Day — not in the *fulfillment* of victory, but in the *assurance* of victory. Christians live in the expectation that we are fighting and working and living in a cause that is destined to prevail. Our cause is led by a hero of God's choosing.

The third name Isaiah used reminds us that the human race is intended to live as a family. Unfortunately, we have learned to distinguish ourselves from one another by focusing on our differences.

We focus on religious differences and create the divisions that are tearing apart our world. We emphasize our political differences and create one-sided tyrannies, such as exist in much of Africa. We focus on ethnic differences and create the genocide that occurred in Bosnia.

To such people as we are, Isaiah proclaimed the coming of one who may be called everlasting Father. What he was describing was someone who could unite us into one family and help us to focus on those things that unite us. Martin Luther King said, "I have a dream," a dream of black and white children playing together unhindered by racial difference. Those who followed him shared that dream, and they sang "We Shall Overcome" — not overcome other people, but overcome what divides us. Two women stood on the fringes of a peace rally in Belfast cynically jeering and laughing at the idea of a peace march. Both had lost their husbands in the sectarian violence that divided their land. They were filled with bitterness. One was Protestant, the other was Catholic. They were shocked to discover that, despite their differences, they could agree on the stupidity of the peace march. As they watched, their attention was drawn to an old man holding high a beautifully carved dove with the word "peace" chiseled into the wood below. As they talked with him, they learned that he was looking for someone to carry the dove to all the peace marches. He was too old and ill to make the journey. Yet he wanted the dove to be carried on high as a symbol of his forgiveness of the death of his son, who had been shot in the sectarian violence two weeks before. The two women were so moved by the compassion of this stranger that they agreed to bear witness in his place. Their participation in the march that day was tinged with a hope that became a fierce commitment. They carried the dove across Northern Ireland to every peace rally. In the process they became firm friends and their example gave other people the courage to stand together for peace and justice. On the night of his betrayal, Jesus prayed for his followers that they might be one, even as he and the Father were one. And if there is one Father, there is one family.

The fourth name Isaiah used focuses on our desire to live in an era of peace among the nations. The history of our race seems to be one of unending conflict. I have books in my own library with such titles as *The Gallic Wars*, *The Punic Wars*, *The Iliad*, which memorializes the Trojan War, a six-volume set by Churchill, titled *The Second World War* and others of similar material. War punctuates every era of human history and makes us wonder if it can be any other way.

As Henry Wadsworth Longfellow was listening to the ringing of the Christmas bells in Cambridge, Massachusetts, in 1863, deep feelings and memories began to stir within him. It had been only six months since the Battle of Gettysburg. The nation was mourning the death of so many loved ones during the Civil War. Longfellow's own young son had been wounded. His thoughts turned to peace. The words from Luke "... peace on earth, goodwill toward men," inspired him to write his well-beloved poem:

I heard the bells on Christmas Day their old familiar carol play,
And wild and sweet the words repeat
Of peace on earth, good-will to men! And thought how, as the day had come,
The belfries of all Christendom had rolled along
The unbroken song of peace on earth, good-will to men!
And in despair, I bowed my head;
"There is no peace on earth," I said,
"For hate is strong and mocks the song
Of peace on earth, good will to men!"
Then pealed the bells more loud and deep,
"God is not dead, nor doth he sleep. The wrong shall fail,
The right prevail, with peace on earth, good will to men!"
(Henry Wadsworth Longfellow, 1863, "Christmas Bells")

The child called the Prince of Peace came to reconcile us to God and to one another.

To leave this child with four names back in Bethlehem, however, is to act as though he never lived. He is the decisive child to be born into the world. But whether or not anyone is decisive depends on us. Johann Sebastian Bach may have been decisive in the realm of music, but there are many people to whom Bach might just as well never have been born. How decisive Christ is for the world depends on what he is in your life and in mine.

www.ingramcontent.com/pod-product-compliance
Lightning Source LLC
Chambersburg PA
CBHW071720090426
42738CB00009B/1832